THE REAL ESTATE PEOPLE

THE REAL ESTATE PEOPLE

Top Salespersons, Brokers, and Realtors Share the Secrets of Their Success

ROBERT L. SHOOK

1817

HARPER & ROW, PUBLISHERS, New York

Cambridge, Hagerstown, Philadelphia, San Francisco
London, Mexico City, São Paulo, Sydney

FIRST EDITION

Designer: Sidney Feinberg

Library of Congress Cataloging in Publication Data

Shook, Robert L   1938–
   The real estate people.

   1. Real estate agents—United States—Interviews.
2. Real estate business—United States. I. Title.
HD255.S56 1980   333.33′092′2   80–7599
ISBN 0-06-014038-0

80 81 82 83 10 9 8 7 6 5 4 3 2 1

To my daughter, Carrie, with love

Acknowledgments

To Rosemarie Bailey, Roger Benjamin, Nancy Cone, Whit Dillon, Tom Elsass, John Fransen, Celia Fried, Bob Gorman, Donald E. Grempler, Leona Helmsley, Irv Levey, Ellen Nash, Linda Neilson, Joyce Parks, Ray Roper, Irwin Schoffman, Jerry Schottenstein, Stephen Schwartz, John Steffans, Janice Studwell, and Susie Westergard. I am particularly grateful to Jeanne Desy, who helped me prepare the manuscript.

I am also very grateful to the wonderful real estate people I interviewed, who graciously volunteered their valuable time to share their philosophies, ideas, and stories.

Contents

THE REAL ESTATE PEOPLE

Introduction

From the time we enter this world in a hospital to the time we exit to a cemetery lot, we are all involved with real estate. Our homes, schools, factories, and offices are all real estate. And the price of every product includes the cost of the real estate involved in making it.

As a growing population continually shrinks our world, the demand for real estate keeps outpacing the supply. Homes, recreational land, investment property—we all want to own a piece of America.

Although Americans are obsessed with real estate, relatively few people understand it. Since it is the biggest investment most people make, it's too costly to learn about it by trial and error. However, you're not going to become an expert by reading textbooks. Most theories on the subject don't seem to stand the test of time.

I can recall taking a college real estate course in the late 1950s and hearing the professor's advice, "Never buy a home as an investment. A home is strictly a luxury." As it turned out, my home is the best investment I have ever made, and I am certain most American homeowners have had the same experience. While the professor's theory might have been correct at the time of his lecture, today's market is entirely different. The field of real estate changes so quickly that some textbooks are outdated by the time they are published.

This book is written in large part for the estimated 2.1 million licensed real estate agents in the United States.* However, the non-professional should also be knowledgeable about real estate. Americans own $2.2 trillion in single-family dwellings alone. And a homeowner who paid $30,000 for his home in 1969 has seen its value more than double in a ten-year period. If he bought into a mutual fund the same year, it has yet to break even. Real estate has been one of the few investments to keep ahead of inflation; consequently, the demand for property has reached an all-time high.

The Real Estate People isn't a book of theory. It's about people—ten of the most successful people in the American real estate industry, who will share their philosophies and strategies with you.

Reflecting the fact that the highest percentage of the industry's work force sells homes, and that the majority of property is residential, six of the ten are engaged in residential real estate. The subjects of the remaining four chapters are leaders in real estate franchising, apartment housing, shopping centers, and commercial properties. These ten individuals are considered the very best in the business. You, the reader, can thus learn from the top real estate people in the country.

Of course, there are outstanding real estate people who are *not* in this book. It would be impossible to include everybody who is worthy of an interview. And since additional chapters on the same fields would be redundant, I elected to limit the

* In real estate terms a *broker* is a person licensed by a state to act as intermediary to bring parties together and assist them in negotiating a contract. A *salesperson* is licensed by a state to be employed by a real estate broker to conduct negotiations under the broker's supervision. *Realtor* is a registered collective membership mark that may be used only by a broker who is a member of a real estate board affiliated with the National Association of Realtors. All these people are *agents* in the sense that they are authorized to act on behalf of others, the buyers and sellers.

book to ten chapters. My selections in the residential area were carefully chosen after contacting hundreds of people throughout the country, many of whom are active on the boards of local and state real estate associations. In non-residential real estate, a great deal of public information is available, and it was thus easier to identify outstanding individuals. Shopping centers, large apartment complexes, industrial parks, and high-rise office buildings are highly visible, and the leaders in these areas are nationally recognized.

I was also careful to select a geographical cross section of America. Although it would have been much easier to interview ten people in one section of the United States, the results would not have been representative of the whole country. A piece of real estate is fixed in one particular locale, and while certain basic concepts can be universally applied, conditions influencing the value of property vary from community to community.

Bettye Hardeman of Atlanta, Georgia, and *Phyllis Burhenn* of Tustin, California, are two real estate salespeople practically everybody can identify with. Both are presently selling residential real estate, and doing a super job. In 1979, Phyllis sold $13.5 million worth of houses—and that was only her fifth year in the business! Bettye sold $17.7 million during 1979—her tenth year in real estate. Bettye's 1979 sales total represents perhaps the highest residential volume of any agent in America.

Gordon Gundaker of St. Louis is another individual who has had outstanding success within a relatively short period of time. In 1968, he started a one-man agency; by 1979 Gundaker Realtors had a sales force of 600 with a volume of $382 million. His chapter tells how he was able to achieve such impressive growth—perhaps the most volume any agency has ever achieved within its first ten years.

Mary Bell Grempler of Baltimore founded Grempler Realty in 1960; today her more than 600 agents have a sales volume in excess of $300 million a year. Much of her success can be attributed to the innovative concepts she brought to the real estate industry.

Ebby Halliday, who founded her agency in 1945, has become a legend among real estate people and the general public throughout Texas. In 1979, Ebby Halliday, Realtors, had 550 sales associates who produced $471 million in sales.

Ralph W. Pritchard is chairman of the board of Thorsen Realtors, the largest real estate agency in the Chicago area. Ralph also became president of the National Association of Realtors in January 1980. In his chapter he shares his thinking as a top broker, and as the president of the 700,000-plus trade association.

Without question, *Art Bartlett,* founder and chairman of the board of Century 21, has been the most successful person ever to franchise real estate brokerage offices. Founded in 1972, Century 21 now has more than 7,300 brokers and 75,000 sales representatives. With annual gross sales of about $20 billion, Century 21 representatives are handling 8 to 10 percent of all residential properties sold in the North American resale market. The company's concept of franchising independent brokers has had a tremendous influence on the entire real estate industry.

Ernest W. Hahn is one of the largest commercial builders and shopping center developers in America. Headquartered in El Segundo, California, his company, Ernest W. Hahn, Inc., has twenty-nine regional shopping centers with more than 21 million square feet of total retail area. The firm presently has an additional thirty shopping centers planned or under construction—more than any other company in North America.

Samuel LeFrak is the chairman of the board of Lefrak Organization, Inc., a New York construction and development company recognized as one of the largest owners of apartment buildings in the world. It is estimated that one out of every sixteen New Yorkers lives in a Lefrak-built apartment!

The tenth chapter is about *Harry Helmsley,* the president and owner of Helmsley-Spear, Inc., headquartered in New

York City. Not only does Harry head the largest real estate management and brokerage company in the United States, but as an individual investor he has an interest in approximately 500 properties throughout the country with a total market value of over $3 billion. He is a living legend in circles where people buy and sell skyscrapers as though they were playing Monopoly.

Here are ten of America's most dynamic real estate personalities. In one of the business world's most competitive fields, these ten individuals have risen to the top. All are experts in their particular areas. And they are all presently enjoying the greatest successes of their illustrious careers. According to them, real estate today offers better opportunities than ever before.

Real estate does not just consist of properties. It is a "people" business. And in order to understand it, you must understand the people who make it run. They invite you to share and learn from their successes.

1

Bettye C. Hardeman

(REAL ESTATE AGENT)

Bettye C. Hardeman is believed to be America's top residential real estate agent. In 1979, her transactions totaled $17,750,000, representing 230 homes sold.

Since late 1968, when she began her real estate career, Bettye has been associated with Northside Realty Associates, Inc., in Atlanta. From 1962 to 1968, she was employed as the dining-room manager at the Top of the Peachtree, one of Atlanta's finest restaurants. She was a hostess/manager at the Town & Country Restaurant in Atlanta's Dinkler Plaza Hotel from 1957 to 1961.

The following figures show Bettye's sales volume from 1971 through 1979:

Year	Number of Houses Sold	Sales Volume
1979	230	$17,750,000
1978	221	13,515,000
1977	199	10,864,000
1976	195	9,704,000
1975	117	5,664,059
1974	118	5,505,000
1973	207	8,694,784
1972	193	7,241,625
1971	104	3,591,604

Bettye was named Atlanta's top real estate salesperson in 1977 and 1979. In 1979, she was the only real estate agent chosen to appear on WSB Television's ten-part series *How to Buy a Home.* She is a member of the Atlanta Board of Realtors and the Atlanta Women's Council of Realtors.

Bettye was born in Detroit, Michigan, on September 6, 1927. She has lived in Georgia since she was a year old, and presently lives in Roswell, a suburb of Atlanta. A divorcee, she has two married daughters—Sherry Bosnak and Vicki Lewis—and five grandchildren: Kimberly, Lisa, Sasha, Cade, and Tony.

With residential sales exceeding $17.5 million in 1979, Bettye Hardeman ranks as one of America's greatest salespersons. Yet when she began her career with Northside Realty in 1968, it was very doubtful whether she would make the grade at all as a real estate agent.

"I didn't complete a sale for my first five months," the attractive, auburn-haired woman confesses. "In fact, I did write thirteen contracts during that period, but for one reason or another I couldn't get any of them through. Finally, at the end of my first five months, I sold a $19,000 house. It was another real estate firm's listing, so I ended up with 60 percent of Northside's 3 percent share. That meant I had earned just a little over $300 for a five-month period.

"But once I made my first sale, nothing could stop me," Bettye goes on in her pronounced Southern accent. "I guess I needed the confidence. At first it scared me to death to write a contract. With no background in business, I was under the impression that contracts were highly technical and important, and they scared me. But after I had written up those thirteen deals that didn't materialize, I had become fairly knowledgeable. I wasn't afraid anymore, and I just worked very hard and everything came together."

Bettye admits that she was an unlikely candidate for success in real estate sales. She left school after the eighth grade and at age fourteen went to work in a drugstore. After two years there, she spent a year as a telephone operator. At the young age of seventeen, she married. A year later, her husband was crippled in an automobile accident, and she cared for him along with her two young daughters. In 1956, she was divorced. She then worked as a hostess for two of Atlanta's finer restaurants for several years.

"I had a great desire to sell real estate," Bettye recalls. "In fact, I had been licensed since the early fifties, but I was never in a financial position to take the plunge until my daughters were grown. Since my ex-husband was confined to a wheelchair, I never received alimony or child support for my daughters, so I just couldn't afford to work on a straight commission while they were still at home. But I held on to my license all those years, knowing that someday I was going to sell real estate. And I did, didn't I?"

Her big brown eyes look thoughtful. "I had $1,700 in the bank when I started at Northside on November 1, 1968. I remember that date, because that's the day my ex-husband was killed in an automobile accident.

"To get started, I moved in with my parents. I decided that I would stay in the business until my $1,700 ran out, and believe me, it almost did before I made my first sale! My advice to anybody just entering the business is to have enough savings to last for at least a year. I did end up staying with my parents for my first two years in the business.

"But I always knew I'd succeed, even when I wasn't selling anything," Bettye says in a soft but determined voice. "I knew I'd win because I was working so hard and doing so many things right. Sooner or later everything had to come together. I just had to stick it out, that's all."

Her winning smile vanishes, and she says in a serious tone,

© *Gittings*

BETTYE C. HARDEMAN

"If I were asked to give advice to someone just starting in real estate, I'd say, 'Just stay in there and work, and if you do, you're going to make it.' Too many people get discouraged easily and quit. . . . If they were just willing to put enough time and effort into their real estate career, they could make a success of it.

"I guess I'd better qualify that by adding that a real estate person really has to like people," she adds. "You can't see dollar signs in this business; you have to think in terms of what's best for your client. Agents should never be counting their money. Instead, they should count the service they're giving the client. If you're doing the right thing by your client, the money will eventually be there.

"I'm always 100 percent honest with people, and they know it, and they trust me. They realize that I sincerely want to help them. I suppose wanting to serve people is just my nature. Or perhaps I developed this attitude working as a hostess in the restaurant business. However I got this way, I'm definitely a service-oriented person. *I'm proud to serve people.* I like to do a good job for them, and I feel good when they're happy with me. I think people know when you care, and I do truly care."

Bettye's warmth is radiant, and her clients must love her as much as she obviously loves them. *"I'm a toucher!"* she explains. "Maybe that's bad, but I keep putting my hands on people when I talk. I just can't help it. I'm one of those people who is always touching other people." She talks with her hands, too—even when she's on the telephone. The overall effect is one of lively enthusiasm.

Throwing her hands in the air, Bettye smiles. "I'm constantly being told, 'No one would ever believe you could sell real estate if they didn't know better!' Clients tell me, 'You're really a different kind of salesperson, Bettye.' And other agents say that I don't go by any of the rules. Everybody tells me I'm different."

When Bettye's clients tell her such things, it may be one of the finest compliments in disguise a salesperson can receive. Although she's unaware of it, she's being told, "I can trust you, Bettye. *I feel comfortable with you.*" The fact is that most people feel uncomfortable in a salesperson-customer relationship because they sense a certain degree of self-interest on the part of the seller. But Bettye's interest is in her *customer.* Perhaps the very thing that makes her a super salesperson is that she doesn't come across as one. Her naturalness is so relaxing that the client feels good about doing business with her. She radiates sincerity. And people are obviously receptive toward the genuine warmth she has for them!

"I only look for good in people," she explains, "and never think bad about anyone. I trust people, and I believe they recognize this trust and don't want to disappoint me. I suppose I learned this attitude from my mother. She had a very hard life, as hard as anyone I have ever seen, but she always had a warm smile and never got discouraged. If she had, she couldn't have raised seven children the way she did. She was always a happy person, and so am I. Happiness, of course, is a state of mind.

"I've had my share of hardships—we all do—but I believe it has made me a better person. I can *feel* for the man who doesn't have enough food on his table. My mother used to say, 'Oh, if I could only have done more for you all when you were younger.' I would tell her, 'I'm glad I grew up like I did. I wouldn't have the feeling I have for other people if I hadn't.' "

It was unquestionably Bettye's positive outlook on life that sustained her for her first months in real estate. During the 1974 recession she needed this inner strength again as her sales slumped from her 1973 volume of $8.6 million to $5.5 million, and the number of houses sold fell from 207 to 118. "Actually, I thought I did very well in 1974," she says with a confident smile. "It didn't bother me to see my personal production fall. What *did* bother me was seeing so many people out of work, and being unable to sell their homes as quickly as they needed. Because there were so many homes on the market, and people weren't being transferred to Atlanta, we couldn't move property as fast as usual. And people weren't selling their houses to buy another house, they were selling because they needed the money! It bothered me to see my clients worry that way. But my production? I wasn't concerned about my personal income being down. I still made enough to live on."

Bettye's number one priority is real estate. She has sacrificed her personal life to serve her clients. "My social life is nothing; my work comes first," the dynamic woman insists. "In this business, you've got to go when your clients want to go. Unless I absolutely have to attend or I'll disappoint somebody, I will pass on a cocktail party, a dinner, a wedding, practically anything, to show a home to a client. My friends understand how I feel about my work, and they know that I may be late, if I get there at all, but that's the way it is in this business. It's very hard to plan anything. I'm like a doctor, on call twenty-four hours a day, seven days a week!"

With a look of determination she states, "There are so many people depending on me, I *have* to serve them! And serving clients means showing a home whenever it's convenient for them. I'm on the phone by seven each morning, and I show homes until dark. Of course, I'll even show them after dark if somebody is interested, although most buyers would rather see property in the daylight.

"Recently, I've been taking it easy on Sundays. I don't start until noon." Bettye grins and adds, "Of course, if I have a client who wants to go out Sunday morning, I'll do it."

Bettye works a demanding seven-day week, and takes three or four short vacations a year of a few days each. She doesn't like staying away from her work any longer than a week at a time. She describes her typical working hours. "I'm up at the crack of dawn. And I make telephone calls every evening until about ten, but I don't like to disturb people after that because they might already be in bed. I tell them they can call me any time up to midnight, though. I work on my paperwork until then, and I review my contracts, keeping a close eye on the follow-up that must be done. Sometimes I'll have forty to fifty sales pending, and I must stay in touch with the loan officers to make sure those deals are going to be approved. It's vital to keep on top of every detail. I'm also always in close contact with any other agents I may be working with."

After a brief pause, Bettye continues: "I think one of the most important characteristics an agent must have is the ability to work effectively with other agents. If I don't have a certain product, and I know of one by another agent, I will tell the agent. Or if I have a listing that another agent has a prospect for, then we'll work together. When an agent calls me, I always take time to listen, and I go out of my way to cooperate. I get involved with my fellow agents and really make a concentrated effort to know them. I feel very strongly about this kind of cooperation. Really, we all benefit by it. I can't overemphasize the importance of developing rapport with other agents. Furthermore, I'm able to learn a great deal by talking with them."

Rapport with building contractors is also very important to Bettye. Since approximately 70 percent of the homes she sells are newly constructed, satisfied builders are obviously a major source of referrals to her. "My son-in-law is a builder," she confides, "so I know how a builder works. Builders don't make nearly the profit most people think they do on a house. I realize that the builder must be able to make a decent profit. If he doesn't, he's just not going to be able to stay in there and continue putting up new homes. Over the past ten years, I've worked for about thirty building contractors, mostly custom builders who put up ten or twelve homes a year, and I've established a very good relationship with them.

"In fact, that's how I got started in real estate— working with building contractors. I worked in Cobb County (northwest of Atlanta) which was considered a rural area back in '68. Other agents thought I was crazy to work out there. It was actually only about fifteen minutes from Roswell, but the other agents never went out there, because they thought it was too far away. I went out and introduced myself to building contractors right on the job site. I discovered that they didn't have much faith in real estate people because of the big promises that had been made and broken. Well, I always made it my policy to be 100 percent honest with everybody, and these contractors really appreciate it."

A broad smile flashes on Bettye's face. "I've never had a problem getting listings. And, as anybody will tell you, that's the name of the game in real estate. I didn't take floor time very often when I first started, and I never take it now. I just don't have the patience to sit and wait for somebody to call. I have to be active all the time. New agents can follow the pattern I used and go out there and introduce themselves to the contractors developing new subdivisions. There's business on every corner in real estate. And there are people everywhere who want to buy or sell a house. An agent just has to be willing to go out and talk to people. If the agent isn't bashful, there's all kinds of business out there, *and it's everywhere!* I talk real estate constantly, in service stations, restaurants, cocktail parties, everywhere!

"Although 80 percent of my sales result from referrals today, I'm still out there continually prospecting for business. I sometimes dress very casually when I go out to the subdivisions. I know it's against all the rules in the book for a female agent to wear jeans, but I'll wear them on a new construction site. I'll go right out there with the contractors and introduce myself to them. I'm not shy. Down here we have red clay. Golly, I must have ruined fifty pairs of shoes in our fine red Georgia clay! Finally one time my foot got stuck in the mud, and I left my shoe behind me. Ever since that I keep a pair of boots in my car. And I tell my clients to dress in very old clothes if we're going to be looking at newly constructed houses."

Bettye works mostly in the suburban areas of Atlanta. Much of this territory is still rural. "This area consists mainly of Gwinnett, Cobb, DeKalb, and Fulton counties," she explains, "and it's just too large a territory for me to attempt to cover it all. I strongly believe that a real estate agent does a buyer an injustice by trying to work alone in an unfamiliar county. When I have a client who's interested in an area I don't know very well, I'll get an agent who does know the area, and we'll work together. It's just not fair to the client when an agent doesn't know exactly what he or she is doing in an area.

"That brings up another point," she continues. "When I first started in this business, naturally I didn't know all the answers. But when there was something I didn't know, rather than chance giving a wrong answer I would say, 'I can't answer that, but I'll find out and get back with you very shortly.' It's very poor business to try to bluff your way through that kind of a situation. You might end up giving out false information."

Bettye's conscientiousness is immediately visible to everybody she's in contact with. It goes hand in hand with her concern for others. Whether it's a builder, a banker, another agent, a buyer, or a seller, she always has the other person's interest at heart. This concern is apparent when she tells how she handles a young couple purchasing a new home for the first time. "I always advise them to buy less house rather than more, and make sure to have some money left over so they can enjoy themselves. If they don't, they're liable to have problems. And if that house is all they've got, they're never going to be really happy in it. They've got to have a little left over."

Real estate people are surprised when they learn what Bettye's average sale is. Most people assume that with a production of more than $17.5 million, she must be selling expensive houses. "Actually," she reveals, "I'm now selling homes averaging $60,000. When I first started in the business, my average sale was in the $20,000 to $30,000 range."

What's so remarkable about Bettye's production is the fact that during 1978 and 1979 she averaged more than four sales per week! That would be almost a sale a day for an individual working a five-day week, but of course Bettye's work week is seven days long. "I'm very seriously considering hiring a full-time secretary to handle my detail work," she confesses. "I presently do it all myself, and I have to admit I don't enjoy it one iota. There are quite a few little things I should be doing but just don't have the time for. For instance, I know many agents give each buyer a small gift, but I simply don't have the time to do that. Of course, I give service, and if you do a good job, perhaps a gift isn't necessary. After all, I don't get a gift from the dealer when I buy a new car, do I?

"And, although I believe in communicating with my lister, I probably don't do that nearly as much as other agents do," Bettye admits. "I tell them that I won't be calling every day unless something important develops. I tell them, 'Call me if you have anything to discuss. Otherwise I'll call you once every two weeks.' Of course, if something develops, I'll get right back to my client. But why should I call him to report that nothing has happened?"

A look of concern appears on her face. "I suppose the biggest problem I find in real estate is that I do business with so many wonderful people, and I never have time to visit with them. I do explain how busy I am, and tell them they can call me any time and I'll always return their calls. I think they understand my situation, so it's really not too much of a problem. It's just one of the drawbacks of working such long hours."

Although Bettye doesn't have the time to socialize after the sale, she does take time to provide services for her clients *during the sale.* "I go out of my way with people who are new in the Atlanta area," she explains. "I take them to the local stores where they can choose their carpeting, wall decorations, or light fixtures. If need be, I get their utilities turned on. I direct them with any information they might need.

"I also like to show out-of-towners several different communities they might want to consider. I don't believe the real estate agent should decide what area of Atlanta *might* be right! I think it's only fair that I give my clients enough information to make their own choices. I never like to make that kind of a decision for anyone.

"Another thing I believe strongly in is showing a lot of houses. Some agents believe in showing only a few houses. But I might show twenty, or even fifty. Of course, once I feel that the buyers have seen enough homes, I try to narrow it down to a few. You know, it can be confusing to look at too many homes. I'll suggest, 'Wouldn't you like to go back to the homes you liked best?' But no matter how many homes I've shown, I always recommend that the clients not buy if they have any doubts."

Because Bettye doesn't take any short cuts when she's with a client, she works very hard for the vast majority of her sales. She confesses, however, that she does get her share of the "easy" ones. "Back in 1977, I decided to take a one-week course at the Georgia Real Estate Institute in Athens, Georgia. After all, I hadn't been back to school since getting my license in 1954. Well, I saw this agent I thought I knew, and said to him, 'I know you from somewhere, but I don't know where.' As it turned out, I didn't know him, but we started to talk and he told me about a fifty-one-acre farm with a house and a nice lake down in Canton, Georgia. He said it was a lovely property, but nobody down there was interested in purchasing it.

"I told him I'd get in touch with him and come up to list it on the following Wednesday. Well, on Tuesday one of my old customers from my restaurant days called and said he was looking for some acreage with a house on a lake. I told him I had recently heard about such a place. So the next day we drove to Canton. My client immediately fell in love with the property, and put in a contract to buy it for $134,000. That Canton agent couldn't get over how fast I had found a buyer. Of course, now and then you get an easy one in this business. I felt especially thrilled about it because I was able to make

some money while I was going to school with a class full of
other real estate agents!"

Bettye believes that an agent plays a third-party role.
"When you take a close look at this business," she points out,
"on the one hand you have the seller who's paying the agent to
get a good price for the home, and on the other hand you have
the purchaser who doesn't want a home that's overpriced. The
agent has to be thinking down the road to when the buyer
might want to sell; he's going to want to get his money out of
the house. Therefore, the agent must always be concerned
about that buyer getting his money's worth. The agent must
always go by the fair market value in order to do a good job
for both parties. The agent is in the middle. The seller wants
the highest price, and the buyer wants to pay the lowest price;
it's up to the agent to straddle the middle of the road, and
that's where the fair market value is going to be. I believe that
any good agent *knows* what the property is worth."

Bettye's clients also know something about her that perhaps
even she is not fully aware of. They *know* that she's always
100 percent in their corner. She's willing to put in whatever
effort is required to satisfy their needs, and she's willing to
make herself available any time of the day, any day of the
week to serve them. Although she's not doing this primarily
for the commissions but because she really loves her work and
enjoys making people happy, her earnings keep increasing every year. It couldn't happen to a more deserving person.

2

Phyllis Burhenn

(REAL ESTATE AGENT)

Phyllis Burhenn specializes in residential real estate sales in Southern California. In 1978, when her sales exceeded $10 million, she received Century 21's most coveted honor, the President's Award. In 1979, Phyllis topped that figure with sales of $13.5 million.

She entered the real estate field in 1974, and during her first seven months her sales topped $1 million. In the same year, Century 21 named her Rookie of the Year, and she also was presented Century 21's Regional Top Listing and Top Selling awards. Phyllis sold $3.5 million in 1975, her first full year in real estate, and her sales production totaled $6 million in 1976. In 1975 and 1976, she was again presented the Regional Top Listing and Top Selling awards.

In 1977, Phyllis sold nearly $8 million and was named the Top Residential and Top Overall Producer in North America by Century 21. In 1978, with sales in excess of $10 million, she was named Century 21's Number One Salesperson in a field of more than 70,000 sales representatives. She received the Sammy Award from the Sales and Marketing Executives Club of Orange County, California, in 1976, 1977, and 1978. She is a member of the East Orange County Board of Realtors Professional Standards Committee and has been a guest speaker for the East Orange County and Anaheim Realty boards. She is associated with the Century 21 Regal Office in Tustin, California.

A former Miss South Dakota, she graduated from Northern State Teachers College in Aberdeen, South Dakota, in 1954. She was born in Leola, South Dakota.

Her husband, Bob, is the owner of A-C Meter and Equipment Company in Anaheim, California. They have one daughter, Jody, and live in Tustin.

Within a span of five years, Phyllis Burhenn has become one of the world's most successful real estate salespersons. Entering the business with no previous sales experience, she exceeded $13.5 million in residential sales production in 1979. Her incredible success story illustrates that total commitment paired with a professional approach is the key ingredient for achievement in real estate selling.

"I knew what I had to do, and I did it," she says matter-of-factly. "I was taught that there were some basic principles which a novice must follow in order to get a good start in the business, and having no previous real estate background, I wasn't about to argue with success. You know, too many new people just die in the business because they resist a proven success system."

Phyllis had a varied background prior to selling real estate. She had worked as a secretary for a plastics company, as executive secretary for Hughes Aircraft, and had been a schoolteacher, model, and airline hostess. "Although I had always enjoyed my work," she explains, "I was looking for a position where I wouldn't be stopped at the middle management level. I had concluded that, unfortunately, unless an individual was

PHYLLIS BURHENN

of a certain sex, opportunities were limited in my previous positions. I guess that's why real estate appealed so much to me. I wanted to do something where nothing could hold me back except myself."

While still a secretary, Phyllis took a course at the Lumbleau Real Estate School. She passed her real estate examinaton in June 1973. Upon receiving her license, she interviewed with six real estate brokers. "I chose a Century 21 office in Tustin," she explains, "because I liked the idea of working as an independent contractor for a small office. Since I wanted to get away from the kind of political atmosphere I had previously worked in, I didn't want to get involved with a big organization. I didn't want my hands to be tied, and I wanted to be in a position where I could do as much as I was willing to work for. Also, at the time, Century 21 was brand new, and I believed that they would someday become an international concern. Furthermore, I liked the manager of the Tustin office."

She began part-time, continuing to work at Hughes Aircraft, and it wasn't until January 1974 that she closed her first two escrows. "By March 1974, I had two other listings in the works, and that's when I started in the business on a full-time basis." She smiles. "My boss told me, 'Phyllis, it's going to be tough. I think you're making a big mistake.' But ever since I started in real estate, I never had any doubts that I would make the grade."

Phyllis made her entry into real estate by working a "farm" area in Tustin which consisted of 248 homes, at that time ranging in price from $38,000 to $40,000. A farm is a small geographic area a real estate office assigns to a salesperson as his or her nucleus for developing a clientele. It is an exclusive area that nobody in the same office can work. But of course, it's a place where there is "open season" for real estate salespeople with other firms. "I was told that the real estate experts all advocate a novice working a farm," Phyllis explains. "A salesperson must control an area, and if you don't follow this approach, you'll die in the business. I was convinced from the start that *I must control my farm!"*

Some real estate salespeople begin their careers with "contacts" which provide a personal following. But Phyllis confesses that she was unable to socialize in her community prior to entering the real estate field. With a busy work schedule, including weekend house cleaning and entertaining, she did not have the desirable contacts which often open doors and help salespeople obtain listings. "I really didn't know anybody"—she shrugs—"until I went out and did my farming. This was a different ball game. I was used to being set on a pedestal, having somebody open the door for me. Now I had to open doors for myself!

"I just started out on my two feet," the attractive five-foot-seven woman continues, "and I knocked on doors. I would introduce myself to each homeowner and say, 'My name is Phyllis Burhenn. I'm your Century 21 representative and you'll be seeing a lot of me. Once a month I'll be around with a new shopping pad and a recipe for you. I'll also be putting out a newsletter just for the people in this area. It will be about you, your family, your neighbors, and the homes in this area.'

"It took me about four days to introduce myself to everyone in my farming area during my first round," she recalls. "And on the second time around I got my first listing. I was ecstatic! I wanted to break open the champagne and have a party. It really gave me a lot of confidence."

Phyllis quickly became a well-known personality in her farming area. Soon she was putting out a newsletter on a regular bimonthly basis. "I knew what these people liked," she says, "and I made my newsletter interesting so they would really look forward to receiving it. It told them the price range of homes selling in the community. It introduced new people moving into the neighborhood, and told where families relocated who moved away. I even included services such as list-

ing the available neighborhood baby-sitters and children who
wanted to do odd jobs in the area.

"I personally hand-delivered the newsletters door to door. If
nobody was home, I'd always leave a note for them. If I had
just sold a home, I'd tell them, 'I just sold Mr. and Mrs.
Smith's home for $42,000. It was a three-bedroom, two-bath.
Would you like to have a market analysis on yours some
time?'

"Soon the people in the area were really getting to know
me," Phyllis says with a warm smile. "During the holidays,
I'd always pass out jellies or candy to the children. On Hal-
loween, my daughter would come with me dressed as a clown,
and on Christmas she would dress as Santa Claus. Of course,
many of the children wanted to have their pictures taken with
her, and we took their photos. I tried to be different, and I'd
consistently get around to each home about every three weeks.
I talked to them, and might ask, 'How did you enjoy that recipe?' They'd reply, 'Say, Phyllis, do you have any new
recipes?' *I was getting involved!"*

In general, Phyllis was well received by the people living in
her farm. She knew, however, that it wasn't likely that she
would be welcomed with open arms by every homeowner in
the area. "There was one woman who was very rude to me,"
she says in a tone of near-disbelief. "I was surprised that she
reacted this way, because her husband was in sales. When I
came to her door, she shouted at me and said there was a sick
child in the house. Well, I apologized for knocking on her
door and invading her privacy. When I returned to the office,
I immediately wrote her a note of apology.

"Wouldn't you know it, the next time I was working my
farm, my addresses were out of order and I called on her
house again! I could have died! She gave me a cold stare, and
I could only say, 'How are you?' Then I fumbled around and
mumbled, 'I'm sorry, but I just got my houses out of line here.
I had no intention of disturbing your privacy. I think you'll

enjoy this new recipe I'd like to leave with you. And also, here's a shopping pad. There's no charge for this. It's a free service.' She didn't say anything, but she took it. After that, I didn't knock on her door again, but I continued to leave her items. I know that she read my newsletter because she called me, wanting another recipe, and although she didn't identify herself, I recognized her voice."

Phyllis pauses briefly, and a look of deep satisfaction appears on her face. "It wasn't long after that, well, about two years to be exact, when I listed and sold her home!"

Obviously, Phyllis's tenacious attitude is necessary in order to become successful in sales. Although she may have had many reasons for discouragement, she never allowed herself to be "down." "I knew what I had to do, and I did it," she repeats. "If things weren't happening fast enough to suit me, then it had to be me. So I would re-evaluate everything, take a look at what I should be doing and what I shouldn't be doing. In most cases, I discovered that I just wasn't working hard enough and didn't deserve to succeed. If I lost a listing, for example, then the other salesperson deserved it more than I did, because I did something wrong!"

Why was she such a rapid success in the real estate field? "My total commitment and dedication," she replies. "I just kept hanging in there when other people would probably have given up on an area. I stuck with it and continued to service my farm. Most people drop out of a farming area in about three or four months. They get bored, and many are unhappy with the slow return they get from it. My feeling has always been that if I'm not getting the results, then I'm either not working hard enough or I'm not offering enough service."

Phyllis still diligently works her 248-house farm. And it has paid off for her. She estimates that 20 to 25 percent of her 1979 $13.5 million sales resulted from her farming efforts.

Another highly important quality she possesses is the ability to effectively manage her time. "I've always been an advocate of the philosophy 'Plan your work and work your plan,'" she says with a smile. "I have always been in a position where my time was valuable, and in selling *time is paramount*. I always have my day scheduled. That's the last thing I do each evening. When I plan the following day, I prepare a list, starting with the most important things that must be done. Then I evaluate my schedule to make sure that it reflects my plans for the whole week, and I coordinate it with my month's activities. Too many people in this industry aren't willing to make the effort to prepare a plan to budget their time. I believe that without a game plan it's nearly impossible to accomplish anything selling real estate."

A good portion of her day is spent researching homes. "I'll spend hours looking at multiple-listed homes prior to showing them to my client," she states. "I want to know everything about a home before I show it. When I research it properly, I can then tell my client about every feature, who the builder was, when it was built, the financing, the taxes, and so on. It would be foolish to hit a house cold. Research on the properties that aren't my listings is vital.

"I believe that I must be absolutely positive about what represents the right property for my buyer. It's important to evaluate the area and home carefully, as a property is more than a home, it is also an investment. So far, in every home I've resold, my client has realized sizable appreciation. And, of course, this enhances my reputation in the community."

All this research demands a long workday. Phyllis's typical day begins when she rises at six or six-thirty. She believes that a professional appearance is mandatory, and her grooming and businesslike dress suits are impeccable. She is on the telephone by seven-thirty. "I always do my paperwork and phone calls at home or at the office each morning," she explains, "and I like to be out in the field by ten-thirty. A lot of my morning activity is follow-up work. I'm quite strong on that— particularly checking my escrows to make sure everything is going along smoothy. You know, if the escrow doesn't close, nothing has happened; so I keep on top of them and always get out a status report to my buyers and sellers as well as any other agent who's involved."

Phyllis explains that, in California, escrow companies are used in the handling of real estate transactions. As a third party, the escrow company processes and collects all necessary documents required to close a real estate deal. It also handles services, such as ordering a title search and making sure that a termite report is completed. An escrow company is likely to be an independent company; however, a department of a savings and loan company, bank, or title company may also serve as one.

In addition to her follow-up work with escrows, Phyllis insists on returning all telephone calls, regardless of who calls her. "If it's somebody who might take a lot of my time, and I know the call can be returned later," she explains, "I'll wait until the end of the day because there are so many things which have to be done during normal business hours. Basically, I try to get in and out of the office as quickly as possible."

The Burhenns generally take a two-week vacation during November or December. Otherwise, both work very hard. "Bob has his business, and he usually rises at five A.M. and is just leaving when I'm getting up," Phyllis says with a shrug. "He gets home earlier than me, and after a full day's work he's generally exhausted. I normally go back to the office to do paperwork and make additional phone calls in the evenings. I get home between nine and ten P.M., and it could be midnight before I finish my real estate reading materials."

Showing absolutely no signs of fatigue, the energetic salesperson enthusiastically continues: "I work seven days a week, and *I love it.* Currently, the only time I take off is Thursdays, to attend real estate broker classes. As a matter of fact, we've lived in our new home for almost three years, and I have never used the oven! My daughter does most of our cooking, and my husband loves to cook too. I have a house cleaner who comes in once a week on Fridays.

"Just the other morning," Phyllis jokes, "Bob put my picture in the bathroom with a note saying, 'Honey, do you still look like this?' You see, he works long hard hours too. We're both so busy that we sometimes have to make appointments with each other to get together!"

Looking serious, she stresses with deep sincerity, "I love my work. I *really* love it. I'd rather sell real estate than go to the beach or play cards. Sure, this part of California with its beaches and mountains is one of the most beautiful places in the world. However, I do get to visit these beautiful spots now and then. Occasionally I'll sell a property out there!

"I'm a very competitive person, and I obtain a deep sense of accomplishment from this business. I thrive on being able to help people. I've put many people into a home who thought they could never afford one. Sometimes creative financing has made the difference for a family between owning and renting a home. One young couple, for instance, had been moving from one rented home to another as different landlords sold their homes out from under them. It was pathetic. This couple was always out on the streets. The husband didn't have VA privileges, so I suggested that they move in with mom and dad. I told them to save both of their paychecks, and by the end of the escrow period there would be enough money to purchase their first house.

"They bought a two-bedroom, one-bath home in Santa Ana, and ten months later I sold it for them at a $12,000 profit. From there, they moved to Irvine, and within an eighteen-month period they had realized another $26,000 profit, and they now live in El Toro. I get a tremendous amount of satisfaction out of this business when I can help people.

"Of course, we had a 31 percent appreciation in properties in Orange County during 1977," Phyllis adds. "Even if people only realize 1 percent each month on the price of their homes, that's not so bad. I know that Orange County presently had the highest real estate inflation in the country, but I predict that we're going to see a continual increase here of 10 to 12 percent during 1980, and in the eighties prices should continue to skyrocket. I base my predictions on the scarcity and cost of land. Then too, look at the rising cost of labor and building materials and of meeting the environmental requirements in constructing a new home. It's simply a matter of supply and demand. And like I said, this is one of the most desirable places in the world to live."

Phyllis sells to a cross section of people. During 1979, her average house sold for $150,000. Her largest sale was for $750,000. She estimates that 42.8 percent of her sales result from her own listings. "I believe that service is the key to success in this business," she emphasizes. "Currently I don't take any floor time. Instead, I'm able to generate business through my farm and through referrals from present and past buyers and sellers. In fact, I get international referrals. Last year, I sold homes to two buyers from Japan who had been referred to me by one of my sellers who had moved over there."

Phyllis makes the majority of her sales in Irvine, Orange, Santa Ana, Peralta Hills, Anaheim, Newport, Costa Mesa, and Tustin. Her reputation in this area as a sincere and successful real estate salesperson has become one of her biggest assets. "People trust me," she says softly, "and they are now aware of my track record. They know I can perform. They have confidence in me. I've established credibility with them." As a result, most of her listings come from *people who call her.*

Phyllis also knows the importance of a salesperson listening to a prospect. "If you listen carefully to what people are saying," she explains, "it is easy to understand what they want and to help them find it." Taking a listing also demands concentrated attention. "When I'm listing a property, I stress how important it is to establish fair market value. It's unfair to the seller to price the property unrealistically. If you do, it just won't move. Then too, when a house is sold it's necessary to obtain an appraisal in the amount of the sales price. In order to get an appropriate loan on the property, I have to be able to justify the price to the loan company's appraiser.

"I have never actually asked for a listing," Phyllis emphasizes. "I give my listing presentation and I listen to what they have to say. It's a very low-key presentation. I'll simply suggest that I do a market analysis on their home, and then we generally sit down and work out the figures. I'll ask questions such as 'Would you like to know what you can get on your home?' 'Where do you plan on moving?' 'Do you plan to move up to a home in the North Tustin Hills?' But I never come out and say, 'May I list your home?' "

Many of Phyllis's customers are repeats, often people she has guided in their first purchase. She tells about one buyer who was indecisive. "He said, 'Gosh, Phyllis, this is my first investment.' I told him, 'Mark my words, in two years, you're going to realize a minimum profit of $10,000. Well, as it so happens, I recently gave him a market analysis. In three and a half years, he's made $68,000 on that little home! I really feel good about results like this. This was a case where I had to help the individual make a buying decision. Otherwise, he wouldn't have purchased anything."

When Phyllis recommends an investment, she believes in it. She recalls a time during her second year in the business when she thought a listing was sold, but at the last moment the deal fell through. "The seller desperately needed to sell because of a commitment to a home that they had purchased," she tells, "so I bought their house! I still own it as an investment property. It's in my farm, and I make sure that it's one of the best maintained properties in the area."

Servicing *after* the sale is also an important part of her success. "I always inspect a home just before we close the escrow to make sure everything is in order," Phyllis states. "And if a seller is leaving the area, I take them out to dinner rather than buying a gift because they already have too much to take with them. I'll always buy a gift for the buyer. Usually it's a nice big plant for their home which the entire family can enjoy. During the Christmas holidays I hand-deliver desk calendars for the coming year, and do some special gift delivering to my repeat clients."

Within four years, Phyllis Burhenn has become a household

word throughout the Southern California territory she services. Her name is prominently displayed on FOR SALE signs; and as the SOLD signs appear, the public knows that Phyllis has closed another sale. There's no question about it. The "success breeds success" principle keeps building her momentum.

In addition to the hectic pace she maintains as a top-producing real estate salesperson, Phyllis has recently completed her studies to become a broker. With her excellent work habits and total commitment, she will undoubtedly someday be one of Century 21's leading brokers.

3

Gordon A. Gundaker

(GUNDAKER REALTORS)

Gordon A. Gundaker is the president of Gundaker Realtors, headquartered in St. Louis, Missouri. Founded in 1968, Gundaker Realtors, a firm specializing in residential properties, has enjoyed unprecedented growth during the past decade. In 1979, its 23 offices had more than 600 sales associates who produced $382 million in residential sales.

In 1954, at age twenty, Gordon entered the real estate field as a salesman with Frank Zykan Builders, Inc. He joined the John H. Armbruster Real Estate Company in 1956, and for the next eleven years was their leading salesperson. He was elected vice president in 1964, the same year he became a part owner of the firm.

He has served as a director on the St. Louis Metropolitan Real Estate Board, and is currently a director of the Missouri Association of Realtors. In 1977, he was elected a director of RELO. He has been a member of the board of directors of the Lewis and Clark Mercantile Bank since 1978. In 1979, he was elected to the executive committee of the St. Charles YMCA. He is a member of the Elks and the Knights of Columbus.

Born in St. Louis, Gordon graduated from Christian Brothers College High School in 1953. He and his wife, Donna, live in Creve Coeur, Missouri; they have five children—Kevin, Kim, Dana, Beth, and Amy—and one grandson, Sean Kevin.

© *McCarty Photography Inc.*

GORDON A. GUNDAKER

Throughout the metropolitan St. Louis area, real estate signs have read GUNDAKER—SALESMAKER.

Admittedly, it's a plainly stated message, but it pretty much tells the story. Those signs have become a familiar sight in St. Louis since 1968, the year Gordon Gundaker founded the real estate firm bearing his name. Total real estate sales for Gundaker Realtors for its first year were only $3.5 million—a modest start for a new broker. However, sales soon grew at a very rapid pace, and by the end of 1979, sales production was $382 million! Never has a real estate brokerage specializing in residential properties in the metropolitan St. Louis market been so successful during its first eleven years in the business.

However, the first days of Gundaker Realtors bordered on disaster. Without question, its early misfortunes would have discouraged the average person from even staying in the business. "We were only capitalized with $10,000," Gordon says, "when we opened on January 4, 1968. And we didn't exactly start off with flying colors. There was my wife—who acted as secretary—a salesman, and myself working out of a small two-room office. I had been in the business for fourteen years, so I thought I knew everything about real estate. Like a fool, I didn't even bother to study for my broker's examination, and I failed it!

"Then a heck of a storm hit St. Louis, and our offices were unable to get any heat. With all the snow, we couldn't get our signs delivered, and to top off a disastrous first week, I wrecked my car."

Gordon sits back in his chair and adds with a grin, "I suppose the only thing that kept me in business was that the company I was formerly associated with had told me I would crawl back up the road and beg for my old job back."

Gordon's personal sales totaled $2 million that first year. Prior to forming his own company, he had been recognized as the top residential salesperson in the St. Louis area, with a 1967 production of $2.5 million. This was possibly the highest personal production in St. Louis residential sales at that time.

"We had eight salespersons by the end of 1968," Gordon recalls. "I had always prided myself on having a good reputation in real estate, and when I started on my own, people just followed me. I had won many sales awards and often had my picture in the newspapers. Because I was well known in the area, we decided to use my name for the company."

When asked if he just considers himself a super salesperson, Gordon modestly replies, "I don't ever think I was an exceptional salesperson. I always had to work seven days and nights a week to get results. In fact, I used to see other salespersons doing what I did, and it always looked like they were able to do it in half the time. So I guess it was just hard work that made me able to outproduce other salespeople."

He looks thoughtful. "I have to believe that servicing and follow-through with our clients is really what we built our entire business on. We got the bulk of our business through repeat sales and referrals from satisfied clients. And it takes an educated salesperson to provide good service. We placed a lot of emphasis on educating our sales force; and in those days, the truth of the matter is, 97 percent of the brokers didn't think that way. It used to be 'There's your desk, there's your phone. Lots of luck. You're on your own.' Unfortunately, that kind of thinking still exists today in many real estate firms. But I believe that education is everything.

"There's another aspect to education—maintaining your sales force. Brokers who aren't willing to put forth the effort to train their people usually have a high turnover rate. Those poor salespersons either go to work for another broker or get out of the business altogether. But to benefit from education, the salesperson must be willing. I believe that one reason for the tremendous turnover among agents is that most people who come into real estate aren't aware of how much knowledge they will have to acquire. Once they discover how much there really is to know, then they must decide whether they want to pursue a real estate career or get out. If the broker isn't providing them good education, they're likely to throw in the towel.

"Right from the beginning, our major emphasis had been placed on properly educating our sales force. Don Williams, our executive vice president and my partner, has developed a training department and program that I believe is as good as any residential real estate training in the country today. We've also developed each of our managers so that they too train their sales force at the local offices."

Gundaker Realtors has an ongoing training course for its huge sales force. Its twenty-three office managers work on a daily basis with their salespeople, and once a month a large hall is rented for a company-wide sales seminar. With invited guests, these meetings have been attended by as many as 650 people. Top-salesperson awards are presented to each office's monthly leaders. In addition, a guest speaker is invited. Out-of-town speakers have been paid as much as $5,000 plus expenses to address the Gundaker organization.

Videotapes about the real estate industry are frequently shown at Gundaker Realtors. In recent months, more than $25,000 has been spent on the best video programs available to train real estate managers and salespeople. "Education is a continuing process," Gordon emphasizes. "You can't ever let down, because this is an ever-changing business. If you stop developing your educational program, you begin to slip backwards."

When Gundaker Realtors first began, it held training classes in a local hotel or motel on Saturday mornings. Later, the company opened its own training center with over 4,000 square feet of classroom space. The training program provides a complete education about real estate, including such topics as how to list a property, how to sell, how to show a home, how to meet the public, and how to write contracts. The program even includes a course in self-image psychology. The firm has a full-time training director and an assistant training director who provide ongoing year-round training programs.

Another major attraction for agents is the firm's liberal commission structure. "I have to believe that we are able to attract many of the top agents in the St. Louis area because of their ability to earn more money with our firm," Gordon states.

A strong believer in compensating management according to production, Gordon explains that each of his twenty-three office managers receives an override of gross commissions of his office, plus the opportunity to share in the profit of his office. "Our system of management compensation gives our managers the opportunity to earn good money and the incentive to manage their office as if they owned a share of it, without any cash investment on their part," he points out. "Our managers are managing managers; they do not list or sell residential real estate. This way they are not competing with their sales force and are able to devote their full attention to management. As much as I personally enjoyed the selling end of the business, I got out of sales altogether in 1974. I realized that there just weren't enough hours in the day to manage and sell. The company would really have been hurting for effective management had I stayed out in the street selling."

Although Gordon firmly believes in providing attractive monetary incentives for his people, he insists that when a real estate salesperson is working with a client he or she should never be thinking about potential commissions. "We're constantly telling our salespersons that it's not the money involved, but *helping people* that really counts," Gordon emphasizes. "Over a period of years, I have had people purchase homes from me and/or my firm as many as five and six times. And, believe me, this is where the fun in this business is! We've had families who came to us with only $500 in their pockets, and today they're in the fifth home which they have purchased through us; and now in many instances have $50,000 or more in equity in their property. And the most exciting thing is that once they own a home, they become part of the community.

"It's an interesting phenomenon. If they hadn't been put in that particular home, they probably would never have participated in community functions. However, when they become homeowners, they get involved in education and the school district; perhaps one becomes an alderman or gets on different committees. It's important to note that the purchase of a home probably represents the largest single investment most people ever make. And they're not only investing a tremendous amount of money, but they're buying a way of life. An individual's home is another shell of his personality, and the home will have a strong influence over each member of the family. It's an ongoing relationship. If, for instance, a family lives in a home for a twelve-year period, I look at their purchase as twelve years of a single real estate transaction. When a real estate person takes this approach with clients, I believe he or she is going to get a tremendous amount of satisfaction out of helping people do what's best for them. This attitude is better than thinking about how many commission dollars are involved. It has always been my philosophy that if a salesperson thinks in the best interest of the client, the commissions will automatically fall into place."

Gordon also believes that a good real estate salesperson must be involved in his or her community. At present, Gundaker Realtors/Better Homes and Gardens sponsors Little League ball teams, as many as fifteen different teams each season. And even with his many real estate activities, Gordon is an assistant coach for a Little League team.

Each Gundaker salesperson is encouraged to work a farm area, and at no cost to the agent the company provides a free printing of a neighborhood service directory. "It's up to the agent to provide us with the information," Gordon explains, "and we'll make up a booklet for him to distribute. We'll print up to 200 copies for each agent; that's our maximum per farming area. And we suggest that the booklet be hand-delivered. The directory contains many kinds of information relevant to that particular community. For example, it will list telephone numbers for stores in shopping centers, and for hospitals, ambulance services, and emergency services in the area. Names and phone numbers of children wanting jobs baby-sitting, shoveling snow, and servicing lawns are listed. We put the agent's photograph on the cover, and naturally our name too. It's a very effective sales tool. Recently one of our agents acquired three listings which we believe to have resulted directly from the directory. What's more, within a thirty-day period, one of the listings was sold for $100,000. So, as you see, the directory really does get results."

In 1979, Gundaker Realtors had a budget of $150,000 for institutional advertising. Gordon says that the firm didn't do anything very different than other large real estate firms except for the fact that a high percentage of the budget went into television and billboard advertising.

"Although we have a large budget for institutional advertising, we're still big believers that the best advertising comes from word of mouth," Gordon says. "Recently we hired a full-time customer relations manager. She writes a letter to each of our customers and thanks them for buying a home from us. A self-addressed envelope is enclosed along with a letter asking them to drop us a line letting us know if they have any problems. We want to know such things as did the salesperson do a good job for them? Did the title company treat them well? Is everything in the home in working order? Were there any problems whatsoever? It's not as though we're trying to check up on our sales force, but rather discovering something which, in the mind of the client, may be a problem. Most of the time we'll get letters back from the customer thanking our agent and company for excellent service. These letters are forwarded to the salespersons involved, giving them recognition for a job well done.

"The salesperson can do a great job right through the closing," Gordon continues, "and a minor thing, like not delivering the garage door key, can upset the buyer. The least little thing can create bad will, and the last thing we want is clients walking around with a bad taste in their mouth about us. Last month we did 664 transactions, and, as you can see, there's a lot of potential there for good or bad will. We can have 664 happy people walking around, and that's going to bring us a lot of business. On the other hand, if we have 664 unhappy people, in a very short time that can kill us. So we're very concerned about maintaining a good rapport with our customers.

"We've taken some money out of our advertising budget and put it into a special fund for handling minor problems which we want to nip in the bud. We feel that using this money to create good will is far better than having an unhappy customer going around bad-mouthing us. Let's say, for example, an ex-owner didn't leave a key to the garage. We'll send out a locksmith and have him change the lock on the door. For $15 or $20, those people are going to be very happy about Gundaker, and they're going to say some nice things about us.

"Our customer relations manager will follow up and call every customer who doesn't send the letter back. And it's really working out very well. It used to be that somebody would be walking around with something in their craw, and we didn't know about it. A few months later, one of our people would bump into him in the hardware store, and he'd say, 'Boy, you really sold me a dog!' Today we avoid situations like that because we're following up on every transaction to make certain that people are satisfied. And those very same people who could be walking around bad-mouthing us very often become a tremendous source of good advertising."

Gordon shuffles some papers on his desk. "Look at these. Here's a report that I receive on a weekly basis from our customer relations department. On this list there are two property owners who stated they were unhappy because their homes hadn't been shown enough. Here's a complaint from a customer who doesn't like the salesman; perhaps it's a personality clash, and it may be that the manager will get involved and have another salesperson take over. Now, I pay close attention to all of the problems. When it gets to the point where a customer calls the manager or myself, I want to get personally involved. If necessary, I'll go out and see the customer. Sure, some real estate companies say, 'Hey, we don't care.' But we *do* care."

In addition to the customer relations reports spread across Gordon's desk, there are piles of computer printout sheets. Without question, the introduction of the computer has played a major role in the firm's most recent expansion program. "We incorporated the computer back in 1974," Gordon says in his soft, confident voice. "For about eighteen months prior to that, John Steffen, the president and founder of John F. Steffen and Associates in St. Louis, had been trying to convince us to go ahead with the computer. His firm is a nationally known consulting engineering firm which specializes in designing mechanical and electrical systems. At first we felt that computers wouldn't work in real estate, but we hadn't really given them a fair chance. We just never took the time to sit down and study the nuts and bolts. Then I attended a RELO Intercity Relocation Service seminar in Washington, D.C., and I became aware that several RELO brokers were beginning to modernize their businesses and improve customer service with computers. Later I went to Grempler Realty in Baltimore, who was enjoying perhaps the most success in real estate with computers, and I was convinced. When I came back to St. Louis, we met with the Steffen firm."

Computerized Listing Service, Inc., was formed for Gundaker Realtors, and soon computer terminals were installed in all offices. Each agent is trained to operate the customer service programs. The computer is programmed on a daily basis to include all Gundaker listings, sales, buyers, and sellers. All multiple listings in the St. Louis area are also stored in the computer. The system quickly and efficiently locates and prints out a list of homes available on the local market that meet the buyer's needs and are within his financial range. The service also assists a seller in determining the current market value of his property. Gundaker claims that the Computerized Listing Service is the most efficient marketing tool ever devised for exposing the seller's home to every interested and qualified prospective purchaser working with one of the firm's agents. He describes it as "the most professional and time-saving sales aid ever used in the real estate industry.

"Our average listing is sold between fifty-five and sixty-three days," Gordon says with a smile. "Now, with our computer, I always have that kind of information right at my fingertips." He reaches in a folder and points to a report from one of his offices. "See, this office has an average listing time of thirty-four days. But this office is averaging fifty-eight days. We have this information available on a daily basis. I can also show you the percentages for each office of how many properties it lists, how many are sold, and how many of *our* listings are sold. Right now, about seventy-five percent of our sales are our own listings. That's a high figure, but we're able to hit that percentage because we get all of the information on each listing immediately in every one of our offices."

Gordon pulls out from his desk another computerized report. "The computer is also vital in determining our cash flow. Before we had it, we were operating in the dark. Almost all of our bookkeeping is now on the computer. Information is fed daily into the program outlining what deals are sold, under contract, and look firm. Once a property is sold, we pick up the agent's listing and selling commissions, and we know that the difference represents our share.

"I can't emphasize how important it is for us to keep on top of our cash flow. For instance, the months of December, January, and February represent slow cash flows in the real estate business. We can now project our cash flow on a daily basis, and with this information, we can regulate our expenses. We can also project our cash flow for several months by feeding in the closings on a daily basis. We can then estimate the managers' and agents' commissions, and also such things as advertising expenses, bonuses, and taxes."

Gordon leans back in his chair and continues: "I'll tell you something else. The computer really makes a sales manager's job easier. We can see exactly how much each salesperson has earned for the year, what deals are in for closings, and what percentage of them are his listings. On a daily basis, we can review with each salesperson whether he or she is a better lister than seller and vice versa. We can guide them into becoming better salespersons because we can work with them on their shortcomings. We have every one of our salespersons on the computer, so we can spot their ups and downs by running a computer program on any one of our people. In this kind of selling, it's common for salespersons to go into a slump every now and then. This even happens with our good people. Just before I meet with a salesman to discuss his problems, I'll review his computer report. Then I have everything in black and white and we can discuss facts. It used to be only guesswork, and it was difficult to pinpoint the *real* problem.

"We can also use the computer with our managers. I can now spot-check each office to make certain that its goals are being met. It's easy to check sales volume for each office on a daily basis."

Plans are presently on the drawing board to open four or five new offices and again the computer plays a significant role, this time in determining the feasibility of each new location. "We can analyze an area to determine how much business we're presently doing there, and we can also review what other brokers are doing in the territory," Gordon explains. "With this kind of information, we can make an intelligent decision on whether we belong in the new area. In our early days, we just drove down the street, picked out a location, and moved in. It's expensive to find out after the fact that an area isn't right. And even today, that's the way much of the competition is still doing it—they're still feeling their way in the dark!"

Gordon says that when a new office is to be opened the company will generally use an "umbrella" expansion. "We'll open in the next community because we believe in 'incubating' our offices. We take an existing office which already has a built-up staff of maybe thirty or thirty-five people and a good manager, and we'll equip it with four more desks and phones. Then a new manager will start acquiring people from the new area. When he builds up the territory and reaches the point where it's profitable for a new office to open, then we go ahead and do it. This incubation period serves several purposes. First, it's considerably less expensive, and second, the older office's manager and salespeople are able to work with the new people. Furthermore, there's lots of activity going on, which makes it easier for the new manager to attract agents. Within a six-month period, we're able to start a new office from scratch and have it producing in excess of $1 million a month in new business.

"It's really a team effort, and the older office is quite willing to help the newer office," Gordon continues. "I think it's a matter of the pride which our managers instill in our people. Our agents realize that the more salespersons and offices we have representing Gundaker Realtors the bigger the market the firm will realize. So everyone benefits.

"Another thing about our new offices, we have the best working conditions of any real estate firm in St. Louis. Our new offices are anywhere from 1,800 to 3,600 square feet.

We'll purchase fine furniture, put in good carpeting, copy machines, a computer terminal, and have the office professionally decorated. The complete package will cost $30,000 or more. We really do them up right, and since we started upgrading our interior decorating, we're attracting better people. Our people are proud to work there. In some real estate offices, a customer walks in and sees a wobbly desk and begins to think, Are these guys going to be here sixty days from now?"

During 1978, Gundaker Realtors became a member of the Better Homes and Gardens Real Estate Service. Gordon explains: "Every year a larger and larger percentage of our business is made up of people transferring from one part of the country to another. Our population is becoming more and more mobile. To capture a large segment of this 'transfer market' several years ago we began developing our own relocation services division. Today we have seven full-time employees who develop and coordinate our services to corporations and transferring families.

"To provide more and better services to our local customers and to transferring families, we felt it advantageous to become affiliated with a national referral and marketing organization such as Better Homes and Gardens Real Estate Service. This organization provides us with national identity as well as confidence that when we are servicing a client who is moving out of our area the client will receive professional service from our Better Homes and Gardens member in their destination city."

Gordon adds, "For years we have listed and sold many new homes for builders and developers. Today we represent some nineteen new-home subdivisions or condominium developments. The name Better Homes and Gardens seems to attract customers to our subdivisions. Also, Better Homes and Gardens has developed builder programs that enable us to offer additional services to our builders."

The Gundaker real estate firm is in the midst of a major expansion program. In 1976, sales were $102.2 million; 1977 sales were $196.1 million; in 1978, the company did $295 million; in 1979, their sales were $382 million. In talking to the sales force and management team at Gundaker Realtors/Better Homes and Gardens, one can sense the excitement in the air. Most often heard are comments like "We just can't believe the tremendous rate of growth." "It's simply mind-boggling" and "We're doing fantastic things and can hardly wait to see what happens next."

St. Louis has a reputation of being a tough market, and it's often been said that if you can be good in St. Louis, you can be good anywhere. Gundaker Realtors/Better Homes and Gardens must be *really good.*

4

Mary Bell Grempler

(GREMPLER REALTY, INC.)

Mary Bell Grempler is the president of Grempler Realty, one of the nation's largest residential real estate firms. Headquartered in Towson, Maryland, Grempler Realty was founded by Mary Bell in 1960. The firm's sales volume exceeds $300 million, and it has more than 600 agents.

In addition to its residential sales, the company's business includes commercial and land development. The firm owns a mortgage company, Free State Mortgage Company; an insurance agency, D. E. Grempler Insurance Company; a title insurance company, Title Company of Maryland; and a computer service company, Data Base Management, Inc.

Mary Bell entered real estate in 1955 as a part-time agent and after five years began her own company, Donald E. Grempler Realty (later renamed Grempler Realty, Inc.).

In 1962, Mary Bell started the Women's Council of Real Estate in Baltimore and was named its first president. A member of the Real Estate Board of Greater Baltimore since 1960, she has served on many of its committees and several terms on its board. She is a past board member of the Maryland Association of Realtors, the National Association of Realtors, and the Marketing Institute. In 1975, she was the president of Multiple Listing Service of Baltimore.

In 1967, Mary Bell was named Towsontowne Woman of the Year. The Towson branch of the American Association of University Women chose her as one of Baltimore County's forty most outstanding women for the period of 1930 to 1975. Her accomplishments include serving on the president's advisory board of Notre Dame College, receiving the American Salesmaster Award, and working on the Baltimore Neighborhood Fair Housing Committee.

Mary Bell is a member of the Board of Realtors in seven Maryland counties. She is a vice president of CICHA (Commerce and Industry Combined Health Appeal) and serves on the executive and nominating committees. She is a member of the housing committee of Baltimore City's Regional Planning Council and the foundation board of Towson State University. In addition, she is on the board of directors of the non-profit relocation service RELO, and serves as regional vice president. Currently, she is also serving on the Technical Advisory Committee of Baltimore County, the Baltimore County Landmarks Preservation Commission, and the board of directors and the executive committee of the Greater Baltimore Board of Realtors. Since 1977, she has been a member of the board of directors of the Baltimore Symphony, an indication of her diversified interests.

Mary Bell was born on March 30, 1931, in Devlin, Ontario. She graduated from the school of nursing at Montana State College in 1952. With her husband, Donald, and two sons, Donald R. and Jimmy, she now lives in Stevenson, Maryland.

Several years ago, Mary Bell Grempler and her husband were on their way to Ocean City for a weekend vacation. "You know, Don," Mary Bell remarked with a sigh, her mind still obviously on real estate, "wouldn't it be nice if there were a machine packed with information on properties, and all you had to do was to push the buttons and the listings would come out!"

She was kidding, but Donald pondered for a moment and replied, "That shouldn't be so difficult, honey." When they returned from vacation, he immediately began work on a computer program to furnish instant information on real estate inventories.

The Gremplers thereby introduced an innovative concept to the real estate industry, and, in the process, Grempler Realty became one of the nation's largest real estate firms. Today there are twelve regional Grempler offices built specifically for real estate and strategically located throughout Maryland. Each office, consisting of over 4,000 square feet, is fully computerized, and the combined sales force of more than 600 agents is equipped to offer a complete array of in-house services, ranging from title insurance to obtaining mortgage money through Grempler subsidiary companies. The firm's computer service system is believed to be the most sophisticated program in the United States dealing with residential properties.

What kind of woman does one expect to run an awesome real estate company consisting of computers, a title insurance company, and a mortgage company coupled with a huge army of sales agents? You might visualize an overpowering executive puffing a slim cigar. If so, then you'd be quite surprised to meet Mary Bell, a trim, attractive woman who looks considerably younger than her forty-eight years. The Canadian-born, Montana-raised ex-nurse still possesses the same down-to-earth qualities she had prior to becoming one of America's most successful real estate entrepreneurs.

She met Donald, an Air Force pilot, while he was in school in Great Falls, Montana. He courted her during layovers on trips from San Antonio to Alaska. The couple married and moved to his hometown, Baltimore.

"When we first lived in Baltimore," Mary Bell recalls, "Don was a commercial pilot for Bendix. In 1955, I entered real estate because I wanted to keep busy while he was out of town on business. I wasn't too much different from other women in real estate. I just wanted to earn some extra money to purchase a new chair, carpeting, or perhaps a patio."

She blushes slightly. "I didn't even know what a deed was! In those days you just *became* a real estate agent. There weren't any courses to take like there are now—absolutely no training. They just sat you down at a desk and handed you a list of properties. Since I'd taught nursing before, I was absolutely shocked.

"When I look back," Mary Bell analyzes, "I probably wouldn't have gone into business for myself if it hadn't been for the fact that my broker was so completely unorganized. I knew there had to be a better way."

Mary Bell worked for a real estate broker for five years. In 1960, her husband persuaded her to open a small two-room

MARY BELL GREMPLER

office. "Don was flying all over the world," she explains. "He had a great job. But neither one of us liked the fact that he was away from home all the time. He wanted to own his own business, and since we weren't wealthy people, Don suggested that I start a real estate business. He figured that with the money I'd make, we'd eventually have enough to support the family; then he could quit his job and start a research and engineering firm."

Although at that time Donald wasn't actively involved in real estate, Mary Bell insisted that the firm be called Donald E. Grempler Realty. "In those days, I didn't want any signs with a woman's name. I didn't even want to call the business Grempler Realty, because I didn't want there to be any question about it. I wanted it to appear to be a man's business."

Within a week, Mary Bell hired her first agent, Shirley Hannon, who is still with the firm. "Shirley was also with a broker who wasn't too organized," Mary Bell explains, "and I stressed how efficiently I planned to run my office. Actually, my first twenty agents were women. I think they felt that because I was a woman we were going to have a lot of fun proving that we could do a good job."

Two years later, she hired the firm's first male agent. "It took that long before a man could get up enough courage to join us." She laughs. "I didn't want to get an all-woman image, so I really solicited some male agents, and once I got the right one, I made him my sales manager. After that, it was easier to hire other men."

Soon the Gremplers moved their offices to a large attractive stone home, which they purchased and completely refurbished. It wasn't long before they needed additional space and built a 16,000-square-foot, four-story office building, the present headquarters for Grempler Realty.

Mary Bell believes that her unusual emphasis on education attracted new agents to the company. "We were the first firm in this area that had a procedure book," she states. "I realized that a tremendous void existed in Baltimore in developing new agents.

"I also believed that my personal production had to be secondary to my concentration on developing other people. In those days, real estate brokers took all of the attractive listings for themselves; I decided that I shouldn't compete with my salespeople. That's a difficult transition for most people to make when they first enter the management end of the business. I found it especially hard because I had enjoyed selling so much. But because I wanted to help my agents, I assigned my customers to them.

"Much of my time was spent in contacting large companies who transferred people to Baltimore. I liked working with these companies, IBM, for instance, because I believed that finding the right house for a customer has a tremendous effect on the entire pattern of a family. I think that most people don't like Baltimore when they first arrive and they appreciate the personal interest we have in them. Also, when we work with big companies, if we do a good job, they refer us to other new people who are transferred to town, and the whole thing snowballs."

Mary Bell becomes serious. "We did something different than other real estate people," she says, carefully choosing her words. "We are primarily concerned with the buyer; other firms are motivated only to get listings. I emphasize to my people, 'Look, we're just new in the business. Let's go out and find someone who wants to buy a house. With the multiple listings, we're going to have the exact same product as anybody else. It's only a matter of who gives the customer the best service.' I think that's our whole competitive edge."

Metropolitan Baltimore has for a long time been a large multiple-listing real estate market, and the Grempler firm turns every one of its properties to multiple listings. "I don't think it's fair to the seller not to multiple-list property," Mary Bell stresses. "If a seller requests that we don't multiple-list, we'll do our best to discourage his thinking."

While Mary Bell ran the sales operations of the young firm, Donald handled the accounting and business end. "There's no way we could have grown so large if it hadn't been for Don's expertise," Mary Bell confesses. "He did the books and he was always involved with the tax aspects and how much money we were making. In 1963, Don was on a business trip to South America for two weeks, and we had a telephone communications problem, so I wasn't able to get through to him. Well, by then we had a fairly large company consisting of about a hundred salespeople, and I was getting very edgy because I had some important questions I needed answers to. When Don got home, we had a long talk, and he agreed to quit his job and work in the business on a full-time basis.

"At first, it was somewhat frightening, because we were used to having the security of his paycheck each month. We had always invested everything we earned back into the business. I believe that strategy had a lot to do with our early rapid growth.

"Don concentrated mainly on financial matters. When he began full-time work in the business, he immediately zeroed in on doing research and engineering to create our computer service. It took about a year for him to come up with our first model because a great deal of his time was initially spent researching what hardware we should use.

"When we first had the computer," Mary Bell continues, "we used it only for keeping inventory. I believe we were the first people in the country to apply a computer to residential real estate. And, boy, did it ever give us a competitive edge! It was something that nobody in our area could possibly match.

"Just think about it. A family is relocated to an unfamiliar city, and although the agent may be a nice person, that customer is thinking, How do I know that this agent knows about everything available? With our computer, the customer can see for himself. He's reassured that our agent is knowledgeable.

"Now, when somebody is transferred to our area, it's not a matter of their company saying, 'Go to Grempler because they're such nice people,' but rather 'Go to Grempler because they have a service that isn't available anywhere else!'"

The inventory service that Grempler's computer offers can

be readily learned by a new salesperson. Each agent is thoroughly taught how to demonstrate what homes are available. Several terminals are located in each of the twelve Grempler offices so a customer can receive information ranging from the price, to the size of the lot, to the number of bathrooms.

"Our first step is to get the customer into our office. We strongly recommend that our salespeople invite all customers in to consult the computer listings. Most agents simply ask their customers, 'How much do you plan to spend on a home?' But most people can't answer that question without having some professional counseling. Some just pick out a price based on what their parents' or friends' homes cost, or they might base their decision on available cash monthly income. When we feed certain data into the computer, we might come up with fifteen different mortgage plans. With those complex government rules and regulations, I don't think any agent could possible have that much information at his fingertips, particularly when you consider how the money market is continually changing. We have several full-time programmers who are constantly staying on top of things."

She pauses and then adds, "We reverse the typical selling presentation because the average real estate person immediately wants to know *how much* the customer is interested in spending. We don't believe that the average buyer can really determine an actual price until he's properly informed about the mortgage market and what financing plans are available. Of course, if the computer says that the customer can afford $200,000, but he only wants to spend $100,000, that's fine. But, it's important to first determine what price home your client could buy under different mortgage rules.

"Once we know the price, we can then discuss the other details about homes such as what area the family wishes to live in, the number of bedrooms, size of the lot, and then we begin to feed this information into the computer. Once we identify certain characteristics, the computer will give us a printout of what homes for sale meet the buyer's requirements."

To illustrate, Mary Bell demonstrates how the computer

works. After asking a series of questions, it is decided that the buyer wishes to purchase a $90,000 home with four bedrooms, a den, a fireplace, two and a half baths, on an acre lot, in the northwest suburbs of Baltimore. These features are fed into the computer according to the zip code of the northwest areas. Then, within seconds, the computer begins to print out dozens of homes that fit this description. Minutes later, the buyer has a selection of seventy-six homes. The agent sighs with relief. He now knows that there is a large selection of homes on the market and certainly one of them will satisfy his client's needs.

Mary Bell then suggests that since the list is so large it should possibly be broken down even further, and she says, "Let's see what's available when we ask the computer to give us the same homes with a garage." Again the computer goes to work, and the list is narrowed down to twenty-seven homes.

"It used to be," Mary Bell continues, "that an agent would have about twenty to twenty-five 'favorite' homes, and no matter what the customer wanted, the agent was going to show only those homes! Then the agent would continue to show the same homes over and over to every customer. It didn't matter what the needs of the customers were. But now we literally have thousands of homes at our fingertips, and we can offer our customers a large selection of properties.

Another advantage is the computer's ability to project settlement costs. Mary Bell explains that Grempler Realty agents give a full settlement-costs breakdown for each customer and thereby leave "no surprises" at the time of the closing. "Most buyers aren't aware of how much they're going to encounter with such expenses for title examination, title insurance, surveys, recording the deeds and mortgages, documentary stamps, transfer taxes, and loan origination fees," she points out. "We believe in spelling out those costs in advance, and our computer service makes it a simple procedure for our agents."

For obvious reasons, Mary Bell is very proud of Grempler

Realty's facilities. Routinely, personnel directors of corporate and branch offices throughout Baltimore are invited to Grempler open houses to view the services offered by the firm. "These personnel directors are impressed with the quality of services that we can perform for their people, and in turn they recommend us as *the* real estate firm in Maryland that's best equipped to do the job."

A "Career Night" is held at the seven Grempler regional offices each month, and prospective real estate agents are invited to attend these classes. A regional sales manager conducts a seminar for a group of twenty to twenty-five people; then there is an audio-visual presentation, followed by a question-and-answer period. Finally, a tour of the office is conducted that includes a complete demonstration of the computer service.

A strong emphasis is placed on continual recruiting. A typical Career Night session includes real estate students, homemakers, insurance agents, nurses, and just about anyone else in the area who *might* be thinking about a career in real estate. Undoubtedly, a lot of these prospective agents walk away very enthusiastic about Grempler Realty's resources.

Each of the Grempler regional offices has a full-time instructor responsible for the development of new representatives. The basic training courses are conducted from nine to four Monday through Friday, and on Saturdays for those trainees who are unable to attend on a full-time basis. Until a sales counselor has completed the course, no floor duty schedules are assigned.

The Grempler training course places a strong emphasis on how to use the computer. Donald has devised a training system that enables a new agent to participate in operating the computer and actually *train himself.* Each training center has several terminals to be used by the trainees.

"We stress that once a new agent knows how to press the right button, he'll have all the necessary information immediately in front of the customer. When you really stop to think about it, look how much faster our people can get started in the business! A new agent can rightfully think, I'm brand new in the business, and if I learn how to operate this computer, I'll probably be more informed than somebody else who's been in the business for ten to fifteen years.

"There's a lot of truth to that, too," Mary Bell adds. "There might be twenty different financing patterns, and even the old-time agents don't know all of them. But, we've got them stored in our computer! First, he's getting instant knowledge on all properties available on the market. Secondly, he acquires instant knowledge about the mortgage market."

Grempler Realty has published two complete in-house manuals. *The Counselor's Job Description* explains everything from showing a house to selling the Grempler system. It also includes details on their "spy system," which instructs a new agent how to properly prospect for customers. It includes procedures and restrictions of local real estate board codes. The *Policy Book* gives a complete orientation about the company.

The Grempler system works very well. In fact, there was once a time when it worked *too well!* In the mid-1960's, Levitt, a large housing developer, became impressed with the Gremplers' selling ability, and they were equally impressed with the firm's reporting and record-keeping systems. "Levitt had built a large project in Joppatowne, and in a nine-month period I don't think they sold more than nine homes," Mary Bell tells. "Then we took over, and we had eighteen sales in the first week! Well, not long afterwards, we had 250 presold homes. Then the county wouldn't allow Levitt to get a hookup to their sewage system, so we had to give 250 deposits back."

She shrugs her shoulders and murmurs, "But that's all part of the business!"

Mary Bell admits that the Joppatowne experience was perhaps her "low point." "Other than that," she says cheerfully, "we have grown steadily since the beginning of our own company. Even during the tight money periods and the '74 recession, we continued to grow."

Each year the Grempler firm has a black-tie banquet honoring its most successful people. Last year's invitation-only affair was attended by 525. She quickly points out, "It's an honor to be *invited* to the award banquet. Unless an agent has a certain amount of sales production, he's not going to attend." There were fifty-seven agents who received awards for producing more than $1 million in annual sales.

This recognition is a result of Mary Bell's belief in giving her people incentive to achieve. "All of the company's managers are paid an override in addition to their regular salary," she emphasizes. I tell them, 'Don't ask me for a raise, *make it on your own!*' So everybody in management will share in the profits according to their contribution. This method effectively motivates people. It's based on my own personal feeling that it's more fun to have an unlimited goal than a limited one."

It's estimated that the firm generates approximately 25 percent of the total real estate sales in the greater Baltimore residential market. They plan to increase their position with continued expansion. "Don and I are interested in future growth in order to provide our people better opportunities. We must continue to grow to meet *their* needs, or we're not going to be able to keep them. If a company doesn't grow, and if it can't accept change, which is something we're always going to have, then that company begins to deteriorate."

Their formula has succeeded so well that Donald is in the process of expanding the subsidiary company, Data Base Management, Inc., nationwide. DBMI serves as a consulting firm for other real estate firms, and in addition to leasing and selling computer equipment, it leases or sells its clients all the software to effectively program their own computer systems. Its clients are located throughout the country. Recently, an interested real estate firm visited the Gremplers from Vancouver, British Columbia, to discuss the service.

"Sure," Mary Bell admits, "there are other real estate firms who are now using computers. But we were the first; we have a head start. It's not only important to have a computer, you've also got to know what to do with it. Some people look at our terminals and they comment, 'Oh, I've seen those in other real estate firms.' But, you've got to remember that some people have an eighth-grade education, and some people have a Ph.D. Well, when it comes to computers, we've got the Ph.D. and our competition has the eighth-grade education!"

Without question, Mary Bell's husband played an important role in the growth of Grempler Realty. Mary Bell claims that the computer is an indispensable part of the organization, and without Donald's knowledge the company could never have achieved its present position in Baltimore. On the other hand, Donald praises Mary Bell's ability, strong will, and motivation. Perhaps it's a team effort and the result of a successful marriage of two happy people who work very effectively together. Whatever it is, those sales figures keep increasing year after year.

5

Ebby Halliday

(EBBY HALLIDAY, REALTORS)

Ebby Halliday is the president and founder of Ebby Halliday, Inc., a multi-corporation whose principal subsidiary is Ebby Halliday, Realtors, a sixteen-office brokerage firm. Headquartered in Dallas, Texas, Ebby Halliday, Realtors, specializes in residential properties.

Before she formed her own real estate firm in 1945, Ebby owned and operated a millinery shop in Dallas. Today, Ebby Halliday, Realtors, is one of the largest residential real estate brokers in the United States. Throughout her career, Ebby has been very much involved in activities promoting her profession. In 1956, she was president of the Women's Council of the National Association of Realtors. She was named Texas Realtor of the Year in 1963, and in 1965 she received the distinguished Easterwood Cup as the Outstanding Realtor in Dallas. Ebby served on the Executive Committee for the National Association of Realtors in 1972–73, and is currently a director and vice president of the Residential Section of the International Real Estate Federation. She was one of the founders of RELO, the Intercity Relocation Service which aids transferred corporate executives on an international basis. Presently she serves on the State and Urban Affairs Committee of the National Association of Realtors. Ebby has the distinguished designation of Certified Residential Broker from the National Institute of Real Estate Brokers.

In 1968, Ebby became the first woman president of the North Dallas Chamber of Commerce, and she currently serves on its board. From 1971 through 1973, she served on the district and regional advisory councils of the Small Business Administration. She is a member of the board of directors of the Bank of Dallas, and she serves on the Executive Advisory Council of the College of Business Administration at North Texas State University. Ebby is a director of the Beautify Texas Council, and the ABCD (A Beautiful, Clean Dallas) Committee. In 1974, she was given the Distinguished Salesman of Dallas Award by Sales and Marketing Executives International. Her contributions to improving the city's environment were recognized in 1975, when she received the Dallas Mayor's Award for Environmental Excellence. She is presently the vice chairman of the Dallas Community Chest Trust Fund. She serves on the Big Gifts Division of Dallas United Way and is president of the Greater Dallas Planning Council.

Born in Leslie, Arkansas, and raised on a farm in Kansas, Ebby is in private life the wife of Maurice Acers, a prominent attorney, businessman, and civic leader who serves as chairman of the board and legal counsel for her holding company. Ebby and her husband live in Dallas.

In top real estate circles, Ebby Halliday is considered the most successful woman in the industry. Ebby Halliday, Realtors, is a huge Dallas brokerage firm specializing in residential properties. For the year ending December 31, 1979, the 550 sales associates representing the company closed $471 million worth of real estate transactions.

It is an understatement to say that before she entered real estate in 1945 Ebby had an unpretentious background for a person who has since risen to the top of a very competitive industry. "I had been in the retail millinery field ever since I graduated high school," the vivacious woman recalls. "After having worked for W. A. Green's millinery department in Dallas for seven years, I had accumulated $1,000, and on the advice of a doctor friend of mine, I invested it in cotton futures and parlayed my money to $12,000. With my newfound wealth, I quit my job to become an entrepreneur and open my own shop. I leased space in a charming old Victorian building, and put most of my money into decorating it. It was absolutely beautiful!" she drawls enthusiastically.

"One of my customers had a very rich husband who had bought an old golf course and built fifty-two experimental

houses on it. They had steel-reinforced concrete slab founda-
tions, and the walls were all poured and erected at the site.
They were practically impervious to bombs! But while there
was quality in the construction, when it came to selling them
it was like the old dog-food joke. It was good food, but the
dogs didn't like it. Well, these houses looked cold and sterile,
and just weren't appealing to the public.

"Because the developer was impressed with the way I had
decorated my shop," Ebby goes on with a smile, "he asked me
to see what I could do with these houses. I took one of them
and carpeted the cement floors and covered the cement walls.
I did some window treatments and put in cottage furniture,
and ended up with what was probably one of the first display
houses. Then I set out to sell it. That was the beginning of my
real estate career. I sold my millinery shop to my head designer, and I was selling homes instead of hats. Within ten months
I had sold all fifty-two homes, and began selling conventional
brick homes for another developer-builder."

A small woman who projects an image of strength, Ebby
explains that when she first started selling real estate her "office" kept moving from one insulated cement house to the
next. "We'd sell one and move right on to the next. And we
went from street to street until the entire subdivision was sold.
I opened our first 'proper' office in a shopping center after
those fifty-two homes were sold."

A broad smile flashes on Ebby's face. "I guess the real estate bug really bit me good," she reflects. Soon I was working
eighteen or twenty hours a day, and loving every minute of it.
Selling real estate is the most exciting thing in the world to
me. It's so much more satisfying to put a young couple into a
home than it had been to put a hat on a woman's head that
maybe made her look a little better. There wasn't any real satisfaction in selling hats; it was sort of a shallow thing. But to
work out the financing and get a young couple in their new
home was a real thrill. Of course, the monetary returns were
so much greater too. I still get just as excited about this busi-

© *Gittings*

EBBY HALLIDAY

ness. Even a small transaction is just as much a thrill today as ever."

Ebby Halliday, Realtors, has such an outstanding reputation in Dallas that today the company attracts new agents without an actual recruiting program. "Our problem is finding space fast enough for the people who *come* to us," Ebby says in her ebullient manner. "We've never had a recruiting problem here. We have never advertised, and unlike many other large real estate firms, we've never had Career Nights."

What attracts sales associates to Ebby Halliday, Realtors? "I think the supportive services we offer have great appeal for career-minded people," Ebby explains. "First, there's our in-house training. The training room located in our executive offices makes use of the latest technology. The equipment includes remote-controlled rear-screen projection for slides and motion pictures, a stereo sound system, and special video equipment. We have a full-time training manager who has two assistants. And we don't just train our people and stop. We have recurring seminars to keep our agents well informed. You see, there's constant change in the real estate industry. For example, we just recently conducted a seminar on the new contract forms which the Realtor lawyers committee has promulgated and which will soon become mandatory. We continually have seminars on financing. Another recent seminar dealt with our interest rate here in Texas, which is 10 percent, so quite a bit of our mortgage money is going out of state. We also have creative financing seminars. And, we're continually trying to interpret trends so our people can serve the best interests of the client. Each office has an individual weekly meeting, and four times a year we have a large breakfast meeting consisting of the entire organization."

A founder and pioneer in the early 1960s of RELO, the large Chicago-based referral service, Ebby believes that her firm's relocation program has also been very instrumental in attracting new sales representatives. "One of the big reasons why our sales increased 65 percent in 1978 was that we handled the relocation of many families to the Dallas area," she states. "We did all the work for several major companies who moved their international headquarters here, and that involved a tremendous amount of people. For instance, during 1978 we coordinated the relocations for such companies as the Associates Corporation of North America, Lenox Industries, Celanese Chemical Company, Mitsubishi Aircraft International, Belfonte Insurance Company, and Fort Worth Railway Services. Our relocation department has six full-time people who do nothing but seek out business with corporations moving to this area. It's a team effort. Sales associates from our different offices work with the RELO department to select the Dallas communities best suited for the company's people. Then we'll send a team to New York, Chicago, or perhaps the West Coast to make a presentation to the company and its people about the Dallas community. The company will provide a meeting place for us to speak to small groups of about twenty-five people at a time. We're practically a Dallas chamber of commerce! We have our *Welcome to Dallas* kits and a complete slide presentation. Then we counsel them on such things as the school systems, recreational facilities, transportation and freeway systems, and the tax structure of various communities. We're able to answer any questions they might have because we're people who live in these communities."

After stopping to catch her breath, Ebby enthusiastically continues. "Our representatives go to these meetings with first-hand knowledge about Dallas, and that's what's really important. We can tell them about the educational system, the church situation, special schools for handicapped children, just about anything they might want to know. Someone may ask, 'Where can we buy a home and keep a horse?' or 'Will my son be able to play ice hockey in Dallas?' These third parties muscling into the brokerage business by way of the home purchase program would never be able to answer as knowledgeably as we do. A local real estate broker is definitely best at counseling these incoming people. We just flat do it better than anybody else, and that's why we get the business!"

Ebby explains why the transferred family needs special service and handling. They need a wide range of information about the place to which they're moving, and often a transferred man's wife and children have misgivings about coming to a strange city. She believes that her company provides a real service in helping make the transition. Printed materials about schools, taxes, amenities, restaurants, and entertainment help the family get a feel for the area. And the new city is less threatening after the family has met Ebby Halliday representatives visiting from Dallas.

Another factor contributing to the company's success is its computer, which provides up-to-date information on the local real estate market. "We're dealing with a very sophisticated clientele today," Ebby explains. "Many of our customers are people who rapidly climb to the top of their professions, often with several transfers along the way, and they're used to moving frequently. They *expect* to work with knowledgeable people. Now, this is why our computer program was such a great adjunct to our business. Since our computer is tied in with the real estate board's, we have all of the listings on all available properties. Our sales agent can immediately have a read-out of what's on the market for a busy executive client, whether the listing is ours or someone else's. The computer has exposed our people to new concepts and techniques. Some associates who have been with us for thirty years are now sitting down at the computer and getting comfortable with it. I am particularly pleased to see our old-timers get involved with the computer. Using it enhances their professionalism and gives them that competitive edge."

Computer terminals have been installed in all branches of Ebby Halliday, Realtors, and full-time programmers are employed at the company's executive offices. Continuous classes are held to instruct associates in the proper use of the computer. In addition to being a full marketing information center, the computer provides faster and more efficient payroll data. A manual containing all properties listed by the company, the *Ebby Book,* is updated on a regular basis by the computer. As Ebby puts it, "We're a service-oriented company, and the computer is a marvelous tool to enable us to better serve our clients.

"Because the real estate business is often involved with legal matters, the chairman of our board is our 'in-house' legal counsel and retains a law firm to assist our sales associates," Ebby continues. "We believe this service helps our agents respond more quickly to our clients' needs. So that the law firm isn't swamped with 550 calls all at the same time, we have the salespersons funnel their questions through their local branch manager. And quite often the manager has had a similar situation in the past, so it's handled by him or her rather than through the attorney's office."

Ebby's total commitment to her real estate career, coupled with her enthusiasm, has spread throughout her sixteen-office organization. "We don't have any part-timers representing our company," she states, "and we discourage anyone from going into the real estate business part-time. This is an all-consuming business. When you serve people, you've got to be available at your client's convenience. Now that might be in the evening or the early morning; it's almost always on weekends. In order to succeed in this business, a person has to be willing to work ten to twelve hours a day. Actually"—Ebby laughs effervescently—"I consider the eight-to-five people the part-timers!

"Real estate people sell service and current information. You have to be in the market every day. Financing, for instance, is a constantly changing commodity. The loan market goes up and down like a yoyo. I don't see how anyone can keep up with it who doesn't spend ten or twelve hours a day at it.

"We have one woman who has nine children. When she was first with us, she had to schedule her appointments around her family. She wanted to be sure she was at home after school until her husband got there. It meant that she was often showing homes after seven P.M. or very early in the morning. I wouldn't call a woman a part-timer just because she wants to schedule her time so her children are being looked after.

"On the other hand," Ebby continues, "if a schoolteacher or a car salesman comes to us and says, 'I'd like to keep my present position and sell real estate part-time until I'm sure it's going to work out,' we won't go along with him. We'll tell him, 'Save your money, continue making good contacts, and take your real estate courses at night. When you reach the point where you're ready to make a total commitment, let's sit down and discuss a career with Ebby Halliday.' We also advise people just entering the real estate field that in the present market they should have enough savings to last them six months, because it may be that long until they begin to generate income. Of course, today, with many families having two incomes, most people seem to have the necessary staying power."

An unusual question is asked on the company's recruiting application: "Do you smoke?" If the answer is yes, then a second question follows: "Are you willing to cease smoking in order to be associated with our company?" "We've been adamant about not polluting the air; we want to protect the lungs and health of the people associated with us," Ebby insists. "We will not knowingly associate an individual who smokes. Now, if a person replies that he or she only smokes socially, well, what's done on his or her own time is not our concern. But we don't want the quality of the air ruined for everyone else in the office. Of course, from a selling point of view, if a non-smoking prospective client gets into a car that stinks of smoke, that salesperson is immediately at a disadvantage."

In addition to its smoking regulations, the company has a dress code requesting that women wear skirts instead of pants while on the job. "We're flexible," Ebby says, "so in one of our new outlying offices where they handle a lot of rural properties, they took a vote on it. They decided to keep on wearing skirts. Their reason was 'We take pride in the company's image, and we want to carry on the tradition that the Ebby Halliday woman works like a man but dresses like a lady.'"

Ebby's enthusiasm and magnetism quickly mark her as a super salesperson, but she thinks good salesmanship is not the only key to success for a real estate broker. "Quite frankly, I guess I was just lucky to change products at the right time and be in the right place," she says modestly. "Of course, it also takes sheer hard work in this business."

She looks thoughtful. "Most important," she states, "we've built a reputation for providing service, and we work very hard to maintain this image. A home represents the biggest investment that most people make. And, while we may list and sell thousands of homes, we must always remember that the homeowner is only concerned about one. He wants to know what's happening with his particular home on a daily basis. So we stress continual communications with the homeowner. Not only is it important to tell him about the good showings and comments, but we must also pass along information about what *isn't* happening. If a home hasn't been sold in a thirty-day period, we'll generally go there personally and reanalyze the property. Current read-outs of comparable properties are discussed. Perhaps the homeowner is encouraged to do some repairs, recarpet, add a touch of paint where it's needed. In any case, communication is the key. Inform! Inform! Inform! You cannot overinform. For cases where executives are transferred out of the area before their property is sold, we have national WATS lines, both incoming and outgoing, so we can call or be called anywhere in the country. I believe this kind of service is vital in our business."

Service is an important theme with Ebby. Ebby Halliday, Realtors, has established a well-deserved reputation throughout the country. And, as Ebby says, "Once you have this kind of reputation, you've got to work hard every day to keep it. You must continually prove yourself. You can have forty beautiful transactions with a ribbon tied around them and everybody happy, but if you fall down a single time, those forty good ones can be forgotten. We never forget that real estate is a service business. All real estate firms sell the same product, so service is what separates us from our competition.

"Recently we had a man come in who claimed that his pipes froze between the time of his closing and when he took possession of his home. It was a rural property where our listing agent had failed to turn off the water. We had obviously slipped up, so we immediately wrote him out a check for $500. Of course, he was tickled pink with our fast response. I'm sure that some real estate firms would have argued with him, and it could even have resulted in a lawsuit. But when it's a matter of ethics, or when we simply make a mistake, our policy is to graciously and quickly respond. That's something I learned back in my millinery days. If a woman brought a hat back, even though I knew she wore it to church that Sunday, if I thought I was going to eventually have to give her a refund, I'd do it as graciously and quickly as possible. That's called saving a customer! I've seen business people put up a fight first and then make a refund, but in the meantime, they had lost all the good will—even though they had performed a good deed."

Ebby believes that real estate people who live and work in their community are the most effective in the business. She adheres to the philosophy that the people of each area should be served by community associates, individuals who know the community best and are personally concerned about its future and well-being. "I think that a hometown, home-founded, home-owned real estate company is in the best possible position to serve the community," she proclaims. "A good real estate person has an obligation to put something back into the community. After all, that community is his or her inventory. In our business, we help attract people to live in an area and rear their families there. Our vested interest in the community means we have a responsibility to give it additional time, energy, and money. The community's well-being is our well-being. The community's health is our health.

"A few years ago, I was called in by Texas Instruments to discuss the move of a certain department. I was asked by a fine young executive, 'Aside from your company being the leading real estate firm in town, do you know why I called you, Ebby?' I told him that I'd like to know, and he explained, 'I used to play on your baseball team when I was a kid.' Now, it's quite exciting to hear remarks like that, even though it does age me!"

For almost thirty years the company has sponsored young people's sports teams. In addition to teams in baseball, basketball, football, hockey, soccer, and volleyball, the firm has sponsored swimming events, wrestling tournaments, rifle meets, and model airplane races. "We're big on little folks," Ebby remarks. "We believe the community is stronger when the kids are off the streets and interested in sports. And, of course, the youngsters are the citizens of the future. Now we're onto the second generation." She beams.

Ebby personally practices her belief in community service. About one-third of her workday, which begins around six each morning, and ends around ten-thirty at night, is devoted to community work. In addition, she makes numerous speeches to civic groups and to real estate associations throughout the country.

It's often been said that if you want something done, you give it to a busy person. With her great commitment to the community, Ebby is still very much on top of her business. "I'll always find time to work with my salespeople in the field when they need me," she notes matter-of-factly. "I'll be going with a salesman this Sunday to help him get a big listing on Swiss Avenue. It's a half-million-dollar home, and the present owner suggested to the salesman that he have me come along. I'm always eager to help one of our salespeople in that kind of a situation."

Ebby believes a Realtor's devotion to the community must

be coupled with an aesthetic imagination and an adventuresome spirit. "We must not be afraid to try new things and take risks. As an example," she says, "when we purchased the property for our executive offices, it was zoned for a twenty-story office building. Now, there was no way we could justify constructing our present 10,000-square-foot building on a property with a twenty-story price tag. It just makes good economic sense to build a high-rise on it, but we elected not to, because we believed this area shouldn't have that kind of a building. I suppose I get great satisfaction in making a bum decision once in a while strictly for aesthetic reasons."

If only economics are considered, Ebby probably did make a mistake in disregarding the full utilization of the property. However, she's a woman of both the highest integrity and an unbending commitment to the Dallas community. She is proud that everyone at Ebby Halliday, Realtors, feels the same way. "Our associates are thoroughly committed to serving their communities, and we have developed a valuable first-hand relationship between the communities and our offices. That relationship has taken many years of hard work and dedication, and it is a relationship we cherish.

"We have a commitment to render the best, most complete real estate service possible," she summarizes. "In this business, you either go forward or you slip backward. You can't remain static. I feel that we've built something rather unique in our business. And I believe that Ebby Halliday, Realtors, will continue to be the outstanding residential real estate service in the Southwest for quite some time."

6

Ralph W. Pritchard

(THORSEN REALTORS)

Ralph W. Pritchard is the chairman of the board of Thorsen Realtors, a Coldwell Banker company headquartered in Oak Brook, Illinois. In 1979 Thorsen Realtors's sales volume was in excess of $500 million.

He began his real estate career with Thorsen Realtors as a salesman in 1949, and became manager of the Downers Grove office in 1952. Thorsen appointed him as the company's sales manager in 1959, and in 1966 he became president. Following the retirement of founder Joseph A. Thorsen in 1969, Ralph became an owner of the firm. In 1977, Thorsen Realtors became a wholly owned subsidiary of Coldwell Banker, the nation's largest publicly held real estate firm (NYSE/PSE).

In 1941, Ralph received a degree in mechanical engineering from Stevens Institute of Technology. He was employed by Lockheed Aircraft Corporation as a design engineer from 1941 to 1944, and then served a two-year stint as an ordnance officer in the U.S. Navy. After this he was a co-owner of Pritchardsons, Inc., in Chicago, a farm implement and chemical business which he operated with his father and brother. He attended graduate school at UCLA in 1941 and 1943, and took real estate and management courses at Northwestern University in 1951 and 1952.

Prior to being elected president of NAR, he served in 1979 as first vice president and he has been on the association's board of directors since 1971. His many activities with NAR include being a trustee of the Realtors Political Action Committee from 1971 to 1978; he is now a life member of that committee. He has also been vice president and a member of the International Real Estate Federation Governing Board. He was chairman of the Political Affairs Committee in 1976; chairman of the State Associations Committee in 1971; and vice chairman of the Professional Standards Committee in 1974. He has also served on the Membership, Realtors Legislative, Multiple Listing Service, Convention, Board Jurisdictions, Nominating, and State Associations committees. Other organizations he has held membership in include the Farm and Land Institute; American Chapter, International Federation; Real Estate Securities and Syndication Institute; and the Society of Real Estate Appraisers.

His local professional real estate activities include serving as president of the La Grange Board of Realtors in 1964 and 1965. He has been on many committees of the Chicago Board of Realtors, and has been a member of the DuPage Board of Realtors, as well as an instructor at the DuPage Real Estate School. He was president of the Illinois Association of Realtors in 1971, and has chaired many committees for the state association. In 1974, he was named the Illinois Realtor of the Year. He was in the first graduating class of the Illinois Realtors Institute, where he earned the GRI (Graduate Realtors Institute) designation. He was among the first to receive a CRB (Certified Residential Broker) designation from the Realtors National Marketing Institute, and is a Certified Residential Specialist (CRS). He has been a guest speaker at many real estate conventions and institutes, and has published several articles.

Ralph has served on the West Suburban YMCA board of directors, and is a past president of the Y's Men's Club. He has been an elder of the First Presbyterian Church of La Grange, and president of its Men's Club, and has served as the Crusade of Mercy chairman. From 1950 through 1955, he was a Republican precinct captain in La Grange. He served on the Citizens' Council of La Grange, and is a charter member and past president of the La Grange Field Club. He is a past member of the board of directors of the West Suburban

Chamber of Commerce. For four years he was chairman of the YMCA Boys' Work Committee. He has also been active with the Boy Scouts of America (he became an Eagle Scout in 1934). Currently, he is a trustee for the Chicago Zoological Society.

He was born in Chicago on November 13, 1919. He and his wife, Ruth, live in La Grange, Illinois; they have a son and two daughters and three granddaughters.

RALPH W. PRITCHARD

On August 1, 1949, when he began selling real estate part-time for Thorsen Realtors, Ralph Pritchard had no intention of making it a lifetime career. Like most new agents, he simply wanted to supplement his income from the farm implement and chemical business he operated with his father and brother. But Ralph was far more successful than he had expected to be. "I sold three homes during my first month," the dynamic executive states, "although I really didn't know what I was doing. I just had a strong interest in helping people, and I communicated well with them. I made $2,700 that month, and believe me, that was more money than I had ever seen. In 1949, it was a whole year's salary. I knew immediately that this was the field for me, and I quickly cleaned up my other business affairs so I could become a full-time agent. I've been in real estate ever since!"

Although some "quick starters" are "slow finishers," Ralph has been going strong ever since, and he still gives no indication of slowing down. The Chicago real estate firm he heads today is one of the largest in the nation. With thirty-three offices and 500 agents, Thorsen Realtors' sales volume exceeds $500 million. Ralph has also enjoyed tremendous success in his association activities. Long an active member of the National Association of Realtors, in January 1980 he was named president of this 700,000-plus trade association. In this capacity, his contribution to the real estate industry benefits all its members.

Ralph attributes his success to his competitive spirit. He readily admits, "I am a competitor, and, quite frankly, I have always wanted to be top dog. I wouldn't settle for being the number two real estate firm in the Chicago area. And I seem to end up taking a leadership role in everything I'm involved in. In fact, I've been president of practically every professional and civic organization I've belonged to. Sure, part of what drives me to be president of the NAR is ego; it's a very prestigious office. But it's also something I thoroughly enjoy. And I believe I can have a real impact on the real estate industry."

When Ralph joined Thorsen Realtors in 1949, the firm had three offices and fourteen agents. Ralph began as a salesperson in the Western Springs office, which had two other agents and a manager. Three years later, Joseph Thorsen asked Ralph to manage a new office in Downers Grove. Thorsen planned to establish offices in the suburban areas along the Burlington Railroad as they developed after World War II. "Why should I refer my customers to another broker, when I could refer them to myself?" Thorsen reasoned.

"Our office was a converted ice cream store," Ralph recalls. "That first year my four salesmen and I sold thirty-five houses! That kind of production was phenomenal in those days. Although I enjoyed management, I decided I could make more money selling, so about two years later I returned to selling for Thorsen in the La Grange office. That worked well because I had lived in La Grange all my life. Then in 1959, Mr. Thorsen needed some management people; his sales manager had left the firm to start his own business. By this time I had been the top salesman for several years, so he asked me to take the job of sales manager.

"By that time we had six offices and about fifty agents, so I became a full-time sales manager. Without question, it's very tough to make the transition from salesman to manager. A real estate organization is going to have real problems unless it knows how to properly choose and develop its managers. In this field, you can't bring in an outside person with no background and make him a manager. You've got to go with an experienced, qualified real estate salesperson. However, he's going to miss selling. There's a thrill in selling a piece of real estate—bringing a buyer and seller together—which is almost unreal. This is especially true when it's been a tough deal. Every real estate salesman has had this experience—we all get that special thrill out of selling a property.

"Now, if a person can get this thrill vicariously, and be genuinely excited by the accomplishments of his salesmen, then he's going to be a good sales manager. However, a good salesman is a competitive person, and he's still going to want to be out there selling. I know, because *I've been there myself.* So, over the years, we have always been very careful in selecting our managers. And once they're in the job we make a special effort to make them feel important. When they develop a good crew of people, they get the recognition they deserve.

"You see," he emphasizes, "at Thorsen we realize how important competent management is. We've done some experiments, and we know that in any office the difference between a good manager and a poor manager is like night and day. It doesn't matter where the office is located. It could be the best territory in the world. But if there's a weak manager, that office won't make it. It can even have good agents, and it still won't make it."

Ralph believes that one key to the success of the Thorsen organization is its policy of branch autonomy. "We think the sales manager should be the one to work with his people at the local branch office," he states. "We've built our reputation on being personally involved with our salespeople, and as we grew to be a large company, we've been careful to make sure our management could work with our agents on a one-to-one basis. As a result, we're very close to all our people. We take an interest in the events that are important to them, birthdays, anniversarys, children's graduations. And no matter how big we get, we don't ever want to lose this closeness.

"Each of us in top management tells our sales associates, 'Hey, we care about you. You're important to us. We're not going to make it unless you do, so how can we help you? What can we do to make your life a little easier, more profitable?' And as long as we talk about it at the top, it sifts on down the line."

Ralph shakes his head. "I think this is a different approach than some brokers take. So many are just all out for themselves or promoting their name. I've always been glad my name wasn't up there on the sign. It's too easy to get caught up in an ego trip, and be constantly defending your name, at the expense of your people."

There are 273 different communities in the metropolitan Chicago area, and Thorsen Realtors projects that they will have seventy offices there within the next five years. "In some areas, our offices are as close as a mile apart," Ralph notes. "When we have an office that is operating profitably, we'll expand into the neighboring area, providing, of course, that it has a marketplace big enough to support us.

"We're great believers in what we call community penetration," he stresses. "We encourage our people to be active in their communities, and most of them are key contributors to various kinds of projects at the local level. They may be in service clubs, church activities, education, bowling leagues, whatever. The relationship between real estate agents and the neighborhood is very important. Buyers and sellers feel better about dealing with agents they know."

While, under Ralph's leadership, Thorsen Realtors has become the largest real estate firm in the Chicago area, he is quick to add that there is still a place in the business for the small, independent broker. "Chicagoland is made up of many micro-markets," he explains, "and the little guy can be very strong within his own market. He can be an outstanding local citizen who's very involved in the community and has lived there for a long time, perhaps all his life. Of course, there are many multiple-listing services in Chicagoland, so he can't possibly belong to all of them. When his clients are interested in communities where he doesn't have listings, he'll have to refer them to other Realtors. And hopefully he's going to refer them to us—if we treat him right.

"That's why we place a great deal of emphasis on community penetration. We want to be as good as he is in that market. In fact, if our people aren't that good, we're going to be pretty uptight about it," Ralph insists.

Coldwell Banker, which acquired Thorsen in 1977, is the largest publicly held real estate company in America. Its consolidated revenues are in excess of $200 million. By the end of 1978, the company had 258 offices in 186 locations throughout the United States. But, as Ralph points out, the public wasn't familiar with their name. "They do know who Thorsen is," he says with pride. "We've promoted the name city-wide for about twenty years now, and that's the name we sell. Eventually we'll change our identification to Coldwell Banker, but at present the name Thorsen is very strong in Chicago."

Ralph and Joe F. Hanauer bought the business from Joseph Thorsen in 1969, and it was the company's rapid expansion during the following years that led to the firm's acquisition by Coldwell Banker. Although Ralph remained chairman of the board, he received cash and notes in exchange for his interest in Thorsen. "I receive a salary under my management contract with them," he says, "and both Joe and I have an earnout arrangement which means we'll get bonuses based on production. So, as you can see, we have plenty of incentive to keep growing.

"There were several good reasons for us to become affiliated with Coldwell Banker," Ralph asserts. "For one thing, I found myself faced with the problem of continually putting money into the business for purposes of expansion. While I was building equity, the only way I could get it out was by dividends which had already been taxed as profit. Second, as we kept expanding the business, the risks increased. I've spent my entire life building it up, and I wanted to minimize the tremendous risk we're exposed to as we grow.

"Third, we needed a bigger reservoir for financing. When we were small, this wasn't very important, but as we grew it became increasingly more significant. There's a fairly long delay between the time we make a sale and the time we get paid at the closing. It can take thirty, sixty, or ninety days. In the spring it sometimes takes as long as four or five months. In the meantime, we have fantastic expenses—over $500,000 a month. It requires a lot of capital to wait for a few months until we get paid back.

"Another major reason for our affiliation with Coldwell Banker," Ralph adds, "was their national relocation service, Nationwide Find-a-Home. You see, I had been involved with RELO, Intercity Relocation Service, for twenty years. In fact, Mr. Thorsen and I were among the original founders, and I am a past president of the organization. Relocation has always intrigued me. There's a good deal of mobility in this country, so we're always trying to come up with better ways to handle people who relocate. One problem we had in RELO was our inability to control an affiliated broker. If, for instance, we sent somebody to San Francisco, we were totally at the mercy of the broker's service out there. I feel that if we had a national company, we could control what happened to our customers. In fact, had I had enough capital, I would have started my own national firm. Well, I didn't, so Coldwell Banker was the answer to my particular problem."

As Ralph anticipated, Coldwell Banker's referral network, Nationwide Find-a-Home Service, Inc., plays a major role in Thorsen's relocation program. "In 1977, through RELO we did $50 million worth of cooperative sales in and out on referrals," he beams. "It's a substantial part of our business. We send between 300 and 400 referrals a month to brokers all over the country, and we receive 150 to 200. Nationwide has 700 brokers throughout the United States, and they're particularly well represented in the major cities on the West Coast and in the Middle West. They're just starting to expand in the East.

"Our own in-house relocation department has seven full-time people including John Kremer, one of the outstanding relocation experts in the country. He's co-authored a course on how to set up a relocation department. We have a separate staff to handle the referrals our agents develop; one group handles incoming referrals and another group handles outgoing. We also have a corporate contact man, who spends all his time calling on industry. He's constantly developing referrals for our agents. In addition, we work closely with different brokers I know throughout the country.

"All in all, the affiliation with Coldwell Banker has worked out very well for us," Ralph says with a broad smile. "Forrest Olsen, who heads up their residential division, is one of the most experienced residential brokers in the country. And, although we're now part of a very large stock-owned company, we're still able to run our business just like we did before we sold it. Naturally, we were somewhat concerned that we might get heavy management control on our shoulders, but it just hasn't happened. And, like I said, we enjoy all the advantages that a large national company offers."

The Thorsen firm believes in fully supporting its agents. The 500 sales associates are backed up by a 100-person support staff. This 5 to 1 ratio is considered very high. The company's various departments include appraising, advertising, corporate contact, relocation, insurance services, closing, accounting, special marketing services, legal services, and training.

"When we became affiliated with Coldwell Banker, at their suggestion we hired our own on-staff legal counsel. We chose an attorney who had been working with us on some of our closings and who we thought was very good. He works on all of our business contracts and looks at everything of a legal nature. He also reviews anything that might potentially involve a lawsuit. And we use him when we buy or lease a new office.

"We tried something very interesting in our closing department," Ralph adds after a slight pause. "We attempted to centralize closing. Our thinking was that if we took the closing off the backs of our agents, they could spend more time selling. However, we discovered that they worry so much about the transaction, even if it's being handled by somebody else, that it doesn't save them that much time. So now we just help them coordinate their transactions.

"The branch sales manager is the person who helps the agent come up with creative financing when necessary. If he runs into trouble, he calls the general sales manager. We give our people ongoing training in financing. We have to in this business because of the constant shifting of the money market. Recently, for instance, there was a significant outflow of a couple of billion dollars from savings and loans institutions. If that continues, we can expect money to get tight. So our people have to be knowledgeable on methods of financing other than conventional. We may have to go back to contract sales, purchase money mortgages, second mortgages, wraparounds, or some other kind of creative financing. As a matter of fact, his expertise in financing is the major service a real estate agent provides a homeowner!"

Thorsen's first step in training new agents is a thirty-hour prelicensing program offered on a fee basis. This program is required in Illinois in order for a person to become licensed as a real estate agent. Brokers must complete a ninety-hour program. Once licensed, the agent takes Thorsen's "Fast Start" seven-day training program. "We give them all the basics on listing and selling property," Ralph states. "It's so important for new agents to begin earning commissions right away. Our managers and our training director conduct the program together. And Fast Start is just the beginning. Our agents receive ongoing training to upgrade their skills. We have advanced marketing seminars, special skill training programs, and sales meetings. It's a continuing education program. Each week every branch office has a sales meeting, or perhaps several offices get together. Once a month we have a general sales meeting for all thirty-three offices. Of course, since our agents are independent contractors, they don't have to come, but most do. And we're so big now that we have to rent a hall or theater for these meetings.

"Our branch managers work very closely with our agents. Their job is to create a pleasant working atmosphere and then to make sure the salesmen are concentrating on their work. The sales manager has to keep them motivated, so they're out there showing properties and getting listings. He makes sure they're using their time productively, and he works at generating excitement in the office. Another thing he does—let me emphasize this—is encourage competition in the office. I'm a strong competitor myself, the kind of guy who always wants to be number one. And we try to generate that kind of attitude within the entire organization. We want every office to be number one in both sales and listings in its area. And we work very hard to achieve that.

"We also create a competitive atmosphere among our agents. There's a lot of competition to be the number one agent of each branch and, of course, to be the top Thorsen agent. We conduct several sales contests every year. But instead of long-term contests in which all the agents compete, we hold short contests at the branch-office level. We feel that a long-range contest with an expensive prize like a car has a limited effect on the organization as a whole; after a few weeks, only a handful of agents have a chance to win. Everybody else is so far behind that they're no longer interested. So we concentrate on short contests, a week or two long. In a one-week contest, anybody can be the top dog! Right now we have a contest going where they can earn gifts out of a catalog. And each office is tailor-making sales games for its own people. If an office is weak in listings, for instance, the manager designs the contest to give incentives for listings. These contests are controlled by the sales manager, who works with the district manager. Because everybody can win, these contests work quite well and create a necessary kind of excitement."

The competitive environment at Thorsen Realtors has not dampened the team spirit Ralph has instilled in his people. "In this business it's generally been assumed that you get a listing and then go out and sell it," he observes. "Of course, when you do, you're going to get a big commission. But we don't believe that's how this business should be run. We think a real estate business should be a team effort. One of our agents is a fine example of the kind of cooperative selling I'm talking about. In 1977, she was involved in 108 different transactions; only seventeen were entirely her own. She made all kinds of split deals with other agents as they cooperated on working with buyers and sellers, and her commissions totaled $93,000. We think this is a trend smart brokers will be following. Agents have to be encouraged to cooperate all the way down the line. In the past, many have tried to pull everything in tight and protect their interests in buyers and sellers, but that's not the best way to do it."

The company sets goals for its agents; each one is encouraged to list eighteen properties a year and sell twelve. "If an agent can do that," Ralph points out, "he will earn at least $25,000." And in fact, the average Thorsen agent earned over $30,000 in 1978. Several had sales volumes in excess of $6 million; that represents forty to fifty sales and perhaps seventy listings for the year. It's interesting to note that while women comprise 52 percent of Thorsen's agents, eight of the firm's top ten producing agents are women.

"We're very interested in our agents' incomes," Ralph asserts. "In fact, their incomes come first, because if they make good money, then the company does. And we give our new people extensive training so they can be successful immediately. Quite frankly, if they don't know the basics, they can't sell real estate. Agents have to generate commissions as soon as possible.

"As a graduate engineer, I've always been interested in the technical aspects of monitoring the company's success. So we've developed a series of accounting procedures which provide us with the data to keep on top of our business. We keep all kinds of marketing data on our sales associates. And we have compiled a great deal of demographic information. We *know* our clients—their ages, their incomes, where they come from. Our reporting system also lets us chart the market, and I attribute much of our growth to our ability to analyze the marketplace and trends so we can plan our marketing accordingly.

"We've had to develop this kind of information," Ralph adds. "Although we participate in a dozen or so multiple listing services, we want a great deal more information than those services can give. We want to know how many days our average property is on the market. How long does it take to sell a customer a property? How many days does an out-of-town buyer take to buy? How many dollars less than the asking price does he pay? We can't get this kind of information from the multiples. It has to come from within the company, and we've worked at a reporting system to give us these answers. This knowledge helps us personalize our market, so that we can tell you, for instance, that 87 to 92 percent of our exclusive listings are sold during the listing period. We know that it presently takes the average listing forty to forty-five days to sell. This period does fluctuate. For a while we were down to twenty-eight to thirty days. And there are exceptions; many homes have sold the same day we've listed them. We also know that 60 percent of our listings are sold by our firm."

Thorsen Realtors places a strong emphasis on personally counseling sales associates. "At our managers' meetings," Ralph states, "one of the things we do is give the managers frequent demonstrations of sales counseling. To help them, we have agents give us reports on what they are doing, including who they're working with. If the manager has the right information about an agent, he's going to be able to help him increase his production. Whenever the manager sees that an agent is having a problem, he gets in there and helps solve it. Even if it's a personal problem, he's willing to get involved. Of course, it may be a health problem or a family crisis, and there are some things we can't do anything about.

"But if it's a real estate problem, we're going to solve it," Ralph continues. "Very often it's just poor time management. That's such a frequent problem that we conduct meetings on the subject as often as ten times a year. We're constantly teaching our people how to better manage their time. For example, we show them how to make the most effective use of customers. The agent has to be able to qualify customers so he won't waste his time on those who aren't going to buy. And he has to be able to recognize the serious customers and really work hard with them. If customers are just talking to agents to get an education, give 'em an education. But if they're in there to buy, you sell 'em!"

Gesturing to emphasize his point, he adds, "We encourage our sales associates not to take floor time. Our statistics show that it takes over twenty inquiries on an ad to sell one property. It takes over twenty inquiries from signs to sell one property. Ten walk-ins sell one property. But it only takes two referrals! So it just doesn't pay for an agent to stay in the office when he can be developing his own clientele.

"I've been doing quite a bit of speaking around the country on the dichotomy of real estate," Ralph smiles. "We know that the best salesman is always out in the field; he's *never* in the office. And he's working with the best customers, the referral customers. Yet, at the same time we have an office to run, and we need somebody to take care of the people calling up to answer our ads. So here we are, we need somebody in the office, and at the same time we want everybody out in the field. Fortunately, there are always enough salesmen eager to take floor time because they hope for that lucky break where a customer walks in and it's an easy sale. And, of course, that does happen."

Ralph admits that when he first started in real estate he had some hesitancy in selling a house which, as a graduate engineer, he didn't approve of personally. "For a long time I had a problem in selling houses which weren't perfect—solidly constructed, well located, just perfect." He grins. "I was trying to find the best real estate for every buyer. Soon I discovered that this was an engineer's approach, not a salesman's! As a salesman, you sell them what they want. If they want a two-bedroom, you sell them a two-bedroom. If they want a mansion with big heating bills, that's what you sell them. It may not be good from your point of view, but they love it. And this way you don't get unhappy customers."

In its ongoing training programs, the Thorsen firm stresses three important principles. First, *be accurate.* An agent must be absolutely sure of his facts. A prime objective is that all listing information be 100 percent accurate. "When we quote information to people, we want it to be right. Tax figures, heating bills, lot sizes, sizes of rooms, everything," Ralph emphasizes. "Too many people in this business are careless. They estimate. They guess. They take the owner's word for it. And eventually they get into trouble."

Second, *be service-minded.* Thorsen offers service by following up each transaction and making sure the buyer is happy with the purchase. "If he has problems with the house, we'll solve the problems," Ralph insists. "If it's the wrong house, we'll offer to sell it for him at no cost. We work hard to solve home problems to his satisfaction. This kind of guarantee really isn't such a great risk. It's much better to have a guy out there saying to everyone, 'Boy, did I get treated right at Thorsen,' than to have grousing about how lousy we are. We don't want customers saying, 'Those people don't know what they're doing.' We don't need that kind of publicity. In some cases we have even offered to buy the house back."

Third, the Thorsen professional is expected to *be flexible*. "We work diligently to help our sales associates learn to deal comfortably with all kinds of people," Ralph asserts. "You've got to be able to do business with all types, the young couple who've never bought a house, and the executive who's bought and sold fifteen. And the agent also has to be able to finance both types. We're constantly striving to develop this flexibility in our people. We want Thorsen agents to be known as the best in the industry. That's the kind of reputation we're working for. It's too easy for big real estate companies to become 'body shops.' They're only interested in having as many people out there selling houses as they can get, and they don't provide service. We're totally opposed to that kind of disregard for professionalism.

"To insure customer satisfaction, we've installed a follow-up system," Ralph continues. "Our client follow-up staff contacts the buyer by phone or personal letter to find out if he's satisfied. At present we're selling about 7,000 homes a year, so we want to know who may have a problem. I think there are three reasons this program has been so effective for us. First, the agent is automatically more conscientious, knowing that we're going to contact the buyer. That agent knows we're not going to just let that buyer sit there with a problem and hope it will go away! If the salesman makes a mistake, we'll know about it. Second, the program is successful because we catch small problems before they fester and become big problems. Third, the follow-up call gives us a chance to give people additional service. They may need some help on remodeling; they may not know where to go for carpeting or appliances. Perhaps they need information about getting special care for their kids, or about an activity the wife wants to become involved in. Or maybe they're just lonely and need somebody to talk to.

"There's no question that this kind of client follow-up benefits our customers, so that when they are ready to sell their homes they're going to remember Thorsen. And that is the kind of relationship we want to develop with our buyers."

Thorsen's follow-up service is evidently getting good results. Repeat business accounts for an estimated 35 to 40 percent of the company's total sales volume. In addition, the satisfied clients generate thousands of referrals each year.

"A thoroughly satisfied buyer brings in other customers," Ralph declares. "For instance, one of our sales associates did an excellent job with a client who was transferred from Oklahoma to Chicago. Because she gave such outstanding service, this customer referred twenty-eight prospective buyers to her, and she sold every one of them!"

Because of the company's emphasis on service, Thorsen Realtors isn't interested in part-time real estate agents. "In Chicago," Ralph emphasizes, "where there's so much transferring of employees in the large corporations, an agent must be on call at all times. The agent can't tell the client not to come to Chicago on a certain day because he doesn't work that day! He has to be able to take care of the client at *his* convenience. That may well be a weekend or an evening. In real estate, you have to be available when your customer is. It's like operating a restaurant, a service station, or a movie theater. You've got to work when people want to come. There's no point in opening a movie theater at nine in the morning. Nobody's coming in. They're coming in the evenings, and that's when you've got to be there. Real estate's the same way, so there just isn't any room for a part-time agent."

Ralph believes the real estate field needs dedicated people. He asserts that agents who fail to provide service hurt the industry and don't justify the commissions they receive. As a spokesman for the NAR, he says, "We're looking forward to the time when there will be enough pressure to reduce commission rates so that agents will only be paid on actual services performed. At present, there is talk about unbundling commission rates so that an agent is compensated only for certain services that the owner wants him to perform. This will force the individual agent to become more efficient. He'll be faster and better, so he can earn the same with a smaller charge against the property.

"Today about $215 billion worth of used residential homes are sold in the United States every year. These sales produce about $11 billion in commissions, almost four times as much as the entire stock-brokerage marketplace. Real estate is a big, big industry. And real estate deals with one of the fundamentals of the American system—home ownership. We have to give the American people good service for that $11 billion."

Ralph believes that the future of the real estate industry depends upon the public's desire to own property and the good reputation of the industry itself. He points out that no single real estate company can create this kind of public response, but the National Association of Realtors can. "The association has a code of ethics every member subscribes to," he emphasizes. "This code was established in 1921 to protect the public, to protect the brokers against themselves and agents against brokers, and to encourage legislation to regulate the industry effectively. This policing keeps the business cleaner and helps brokers work effectively together. NAR brought some uniformity to state real estate laws, and protected the public by making sure that every state has adequate licensing regulations. Now if an agent commits an unethical or unlawful act, he can be reprimanded. In some states, we even have a legal fund to pay for the damages caused by any member who has injured a consumer but doesn't have the money to rectify the situation."

By and large NAR serves to provide a better climate for real estate. Of the estimated 2.1 million licensed real estate agents, over 700,000 belong to NAR, making it the largest trade association in the world. Headquartered in Chicago, the association also has a Washington staff of thirty-eight people who scrutinize every bill offered in Congress involving real estate. The staff then informs the legislators of NAR's reaction to these bills.

"At present, we're very concerned about the way the usury

laws in many states are drastically curtailing real estate activity," Ralph points out. "There are states in which the usury law is 8 percent, but the going rate of interest is considerably higher. As a result, money isn't being loaned locally; people have to go out of state to get financing. Of course, one of NAR's ongoing interests is the availability and cost of mortgage money.

"Another thing we're very concerned with right now is rent control. Every time rent control is introduced somewhere, a developer says, 'I'm not going to build my apartment building.' It really stifles apartment construction. And we need apartments, so NAR is against rent control. It's not needed. In the long run it causes serious dislocations. Rents are a very good value. While prices throughout the country have risen 86 percent, rents have only gone up 50 percent since 1969. This is one of the chief reasons why the condominium market is what it is. Apartment building owners are very happy to convert because there's a tremendous market for condominiums and because the rents they're receiving are so low. Of course, the popularity of condominiums is a result of real estate being the best investment anyone could make during the past five or six years. With inflation what it is, everybody has been saying, 'My best deal is to buy a piece of property. At least that will rise with the marketplace.' This thinking has led many apartment dwellers to buy condominiums.

"I think it's a healthy situation when a great many Americans become property owners," the NAR president asserts. "A homeowner becomes involved in community activities, and the fact that he is an owner makes him concerned about taxes, tax subsidies, local government, education, and things of that sort. It's been my observation that he'll be a more concerned citizen than an apartment dweller would be.

"But we're facing a serious problem," Ralph says with a concerned look, "and that's the cost of housing in this country. We can't get people into housing if the costs are too high. Sadly, however, housing has gone up much faster than any other commodity. We're seeing something like 13.5 percent inflation a year across the country, and in some places it's 19 percent. So it's a very serious problem.

"A report recently published by Massachusetts Institute of Technology states that there hasn't been a period since 1945 when a recession has *reduced* prices back to basic levels," Ralph continues. "So when people ask, 'Will the real estate bubble burst?' I don't think it will. I think it's just a matter of having inflation slow down to a respectable level, say 1 or 2 percent a year. But we've got to stop this 13 percent a year rise. Of course, the real estate business is based on the law of supply and demand, and we're faced with an insatiable demand for housing today. Not only is the baby boom hitting the home-buying market, but divorces are causing double homes, people are living longer, refugees and illegal aliens are coming in. Another important factor is the two-income family. Since the Equal Opportunity and Credit Act is now the law of the land, the wife's income must be counted when a financial institution approves the loan. And by the same token, the single woman must also be recognized as a responsible credit risk. This single law expanded the credit market in housing beyond belief. By 1985, an estimated nine million more people will need housing. We have to come up with enough housing to fulfill these needs. But it's got to be affordable housing."

Ralph feels that the anti-housing bias in many communities makes it impossible to keep the cost of new construction down. "It's very important that the local communities stop discouraging housing," Ralph says with a shrug. "These so-called concerned citizens must quit 'protecting the community' by placing unreasonable restraints on new construction. Their environmental controls, sewer moratoriums, and zoning restrictions keep driving up the price of lots and therefore the price of new housing. Too many people already living in homes are saying, 'Hey, I've got mine. I don't want any more around!'

"A good example of what I'm talking about is what's happened all over the country with sewers and water. It used to be that a homeowner paid for his sewer and water mains over a period of years through a tax assessment. Now the builder has to pay for it all up front. That, of course, immediately increases the cost of the home, because it's passed on to the buyer. Bureaucratic red tape drives the cost of construction up, too. It used to take a few months to get approval for a subdivision; now it takes a year. Every delay is an added expense for the builder, which ultimately makes housing more expensive.

"The Internal Revenue Service doesn't permit the contractor to deduct the interest expense on construction loans anymore. It must now be capitalized. That's another factor in the increased cost of housing. Every time the builder incurs another expense, the cost of the home increases.

"The National Association of Home Builders began an interesting experiment recently," Ralph relates. "They convinced the city of Las Vegas to let them build two single-family homes—one of them without reference to the building codes—to be used as rental units. They said that a $25,000 home could be constructed for $15,000 by keeping out the inspectors, who continually come in and say, 'You must change that, and you can't do this.' It was agreed that at the end of a five-year period, if the home which didn't comply with the building codes had deteriorated more than the other home they would tear it down. Of course, the houses were built just a year ago, and it remains to be seen how it comes out, but it's a fascinating experiment. It illustrates how local governments can add to housing costs.

"It's fine that local people have an interest in their communities," Ralph says, "but they've got to be reasonable about it. The barriers they're putting up result in costs that get passed on to the consumer. And when that happens, everyone gets hurt."

As NAR's top-ranking officer, Ralph Pritchard does a great deal of traveling around the country. He estimates that

as much as 60 percent of his time is devoted to association activities. Of course, as a career real estate man he's used to
working evenings and weekends. And having a total commitment is what makes him run and helps him participate in running one of this nation's most important industries.

7

Arthur E. Bartlett

(CENTURY 21 REAL ESTATE CORPORATION)

Arthur E. Bartlett is chairman of the board and president of Century 21 Real Estate Corporation (headquartered in Irvine, California), the world's largest franchisor of real estate brokerage offices.

In 1972, he co-founded the firm with Marshall Fisher (since retired). Today more than 7,300 brokers and 75,000 sales representatives are associated with Century 21. In 1979, Century 21 sales representatives sold an estimated 8 to 10 percent of all residential properties in the North American resale market, about $20 billion in gross sales. Century 21 had revenues of more than $36 million, generated from service fees and the sale of supplies, in fiscal 1979, with a net income of $5.3 million.

Art began his sales career with the Campbell Soup Company in 1955. In 1960, he entered the real estate industry as a salesperson for the Forest E. Olsen Real Estate Company in Southern California and later became a district manager for the firm. In 1965, with three partners, he opened Four Star Realty in Santa Ana, California. While still a partner in Four Star Realty, he formed Comps, Inc., a computerized publishing firm which provided statistics for the real estate industry; upon selling Comps, Inc., in 1972, he formed Century 21. Seven years later, on October 31, 1979, Trans World Corporation acquired Century 21 for $90 million.

He is a board member of the Santa Ana–Tustin Community Hospital and a board member and first vice president of the International Franchise Association. He is listed in *Who's Who in America* and *Who's Who in the World*.

Art was born in Glens Falls, New York, on November 26, 1933. He attended Long Beach College. He and his wife, Collette, live in Peralta Hills, California. They have one daughter, Stacy.

Signing up the very first Century 21 franchisees may have been the most difficult sales job of all time. Century 21's Art Bartlett recalls those early days back in 1971 quite vividly. He blushes slightly. "You can just imagine the reaction we got when we'd ask a real estate broker for $500 to become a franchisee of Century 21. The prospect would look at us like we were crazy and say, 'Now, let me get this straight. I've been in business for thirty years, and this business belonged to my father before me. We're known throughout this entire area. And what you want me to do is this: You want me to take my name off the sign and put up your brand-new name that's unknown, and you want me to pay you $500 to do that. Then you want me to pay you 6 percent on my gross revenue for the rest of my life. You know, Art, you've been out to a long lunch!'"

Although it seemed an impossible task, Art did convince real estate brokers to sign up, and Century 21 grew to become the largest real estate franchisor in the world. And this extraordinary growth occurred within an eight-year period. Furthermore, Century 21 continues to grow rapidly.

There is generally one reason why such a young company

ARTHUR E. BARTLETT

can expand so dramatically in such a short period of time. *Century 21 has a concept that works!* "We emphasized that the real estate business is changing," Art proclaims, "and the small independent broker is going to disappear. He isn't going to be around. Of course, we knew that back in 1971, although the country as a whole was not aware of it. But *we* knew it, and it was a fact. Many regional firms were getting bigger and bigger, and with companies like Merrill Lynch coming into the business, there was a great need for the banding together of independent brokers. There was a tremendous need for the services a franchise company could offer the independent broker. We fulfill that need."

Although a Century 21 franchise fee has gradually increased from $500 to $8,500, Art claims that it's really worth two to three times as much. "It's easier to sell a franchise for $8,500 today," he asserts, "than it was when we were asking $500. And, although the broker pays us 6 percent of the gross commissions generated by his firm, we're giving him a lot more back. We had damn well better give the broker a much greater return, and I would estimate that there are incidences where the broker is getting back as much as 40, 50 percent, and even as high as 100 percent return on what he's paying us."

Art is also quick to point out that if the broker just breaks even with Century 21, then he has gained nothing for the 6 percent franchise fee. "We operate on two basic philosophies. First, from the very beginning, we knew that Century 21 must always give the broker more than we take. And second, there is no such thing as a free lunch! We just couldn't operate on the basis of taking more from our franchisees than we gave them. We develop the same philosophy with each broker and it's passed along to the public. *Century 21 gives more than we take from the consumer.*"

Broker franchises are sold by thirty-three regional organizations representing Century 21. A broker who joins Century 21 pays an initial fee of $8,500 to $9,500 and an ongoing 6 percent of his commission income to the region which licenses him. In turn, the region pays 15 percent of its gross revenues to Century 21. A broker also pays 2 percent of his gross commissions up to $300 a month for national advertising, and each region puts 10 percent of its gross revenue into the national advertising fund. In 1979, Century 21 spent approximately $20 million for national advertising.

"During 1978, our advertising generated 7.2 billion adult impressions alone, through a $12 million TV budget," Art discloses. "Most significant is Century 21's brand-name identification; our advertising programs have resulted in 97 percent of all homeowners in the United States being aware of Century 21. *We became a household word in a period of just seven years!*"

This identification is one of Century 21's strongest selling points. "It's obvious that we're going to generate a lot more business when 97 percent of the homeowners in America are aware of our existence," Art reasons. "The public recognizes our name, and they're obviously going to be attracted to offices with our name on the front of the building. This kind of identification is more important today than ever before. The independent broker is destined to end up like the corner grocery store and the local hamburger stand. He simply can't compete, any more than the small hamburger stand can stand up against national fast-food operations with their tremendous advertising budgets. I think Century 21 is probably the most exciting thing that's happened in the real estate industry in the last fifty years!"

Century 21's rapid growth rate has been mind-boggling. The 7,000-plus brokers who have already accepted it and the estimated 150 new ones who become affiliated with the firm each month prove that Art's original concept, once so hard to sell, has found its place.

Art knew many brokers from his previous business, Comps, Inc., which offered computerized sales and building data to the real estate market. But he confesses that it was even more difficult to sell the Century 21 concept to his friends and acquaintances than to strangers. "Without a doubt," he says with a boyish grin, "those guys were the toughest for me to sell. I couldn't sell anybody whom I knew well. They just thought it was a dream. They'd say, 'You got a nice thing, Art. Why don't you do it?' We never sold anybody on the first call. It was nearly impossible! When we first started selling Century 21, we were selling a dream. *We were selling what we were going to do!"*

Art looks serious. "We knew that the biggest problem in the real estate industry was the broker's inability to recruit and keep top agents. So in the very early days of Century 21, we would offer them in-depth recruiting, and training for the new recruits. In our recruiting programs we'd run full-page ads in the newspapers, and then interview and hire agents. Next we would train them, and finally relocate them at one of our Century 21 offices. While we were doing all this, we were also running our own licensing training program for our brokers."

During the first year, the fledgling company began to fly. Although there was a negative cash flow, 100 brokers became affiliated with Century 21. "We were still operating off of our loans," Art reveals. "I had a very good relationship with my banker from my past business experiences. Originally I only had to put a $6,000 investment into this business, with no personal signature required. We started with a $25,000 line of credit and by the end of the first year we had built it up to a million-dollar line of credit. And, although we weren't generating any operating profits, there was progress being made, with new offices coming in every day. Within the first ninety days of operation, we developed our regional concept, and divided the country up into regions, thirty originally, thirty-three now."

The first three Century 21 regions sold for $500. The last one sold by Century 21 was for $150,000. Art points out that a northern California region which initially sold for $30,000 has recently been purchased back for $4.5 million plus an earn-out.

Without question, Century 21's decentralized system has been a major factor in determining the company's record growth. "Our concept was to bring into the company smart business people with an entrepreneurial desire, the kind of individuals who are willing to work around the clock," Art states. "We recruited top real estate brokers in a given area, and when we sold them the regions, they gave up their real estate business to work with us. Some of them kept their businesses and delegated the managerial responsibilities.

"The regional director receives heavy training initially, and then it's an ongoing thing, with constant communications going back and forth with us. We have three vice presidents who spend a week in the office and a week out. They live on the road, coordinating these regions. Basically, although the nature of these regions is entrepreneurial, their operations are similar. We give them tremendous support, and although there are some differences according to the different sections of the country, we have maintained a strong degree of consistency."

Art emphasizes that the local management of each region is crucial to the development of its brokers. That is why an all-out effort was initially put on the recruitment of top-quality regional management. In addition to the continual search for outstanding real estate people in the area, many of these individuals were sought out by contacting banks, savings and loan companies, title companies, and boards of Realtors.

"The regional office structure is essential," Art asserts, "because Century 21 must be able to service the franchisees. Our regions offer to new brokers a one-week intensified training course in real estate sales, followed up by continuous monitoring of and guidance in their operations. The regional directors establish a very close relationship with their brokers and work with them almost on a day-to-day basis. For instance, a regional director will usually sit down with each broker and help him develop both short-term and long-term goals."

Century 21 uses an evaluation system referred to as "Per-Person Productivity" ("PPP"). This enables a broker to determine whether or not it is economical to keep a sales representative. The regional director will often work with his brokers in analyzing the costs per agent in the office. "It used to be that the real estate business would go by the cost per desk," Art explains. "But nowadays we might have three people per desk. We don't necessarily believe that every salesperson should have a desk. After all, they're supposed to be out in the field. It's possible for an office to have twenty to thirty salespersons and only ten desks. Those desks can float around and be occupied by whomever happens to be in at the time: so PPP is a more accurate measurement."

Another area in which the regional director works closely with the broker is in determining the Per-Office Productivity ("POP"), a periodic analysis of the efficiency of the broker's office. Such guidance from the regional director is very beneficial to the broker, and the regional director has been carefully trained by Century 21 to effectively provide this continual service. The nature of the real estate industry has been that many brokers reached their positions by being top salespersons, rather than by managerial experience. Hence there is a great need for them to receive expert assistance in office management, an area in which they may have had no previous formal training.

Century 21 believes its saturation point will be reached when it has 10,000 brokers located throughout North America. It is confidently working toward this original goal, which should be reached by the early 1980s. In each of its thirty-three regions, a maximum of one franchise is allowed per 15,000 population. "Also," Art points out, "we will not put an office closer than one quarter of a mile to another Century 21 office. Now, that might sound close, but in some communities all of the better real estate firms are located on one main street. And it's important that we have the flexibility to be able to bring in the best offices of a given community. If, for example, we had to go two miles down the street rather than a quarter of a mile, we'd limit our ability to attract the best offices, and it would be a real problem to us."

Art sits back in his chair and ponders for a moment. He adds, "It's a very traumatic thing for a broker to become part of Century 21. Most of our franchisees are very successful brokers when they join us, and, in general, real estate is a very entrepreneurial business. So it's a major change for an individual to take his name off a sign in front of his establishment and replace it with ours. I'm sure most of our newcomers have a lot of trepidation when they first come aboard.

"While they realize the real estate business is changing, and their future as an independent operation is very limited, that doesn't mean they're happy about it. But they know it. Still, like I said, it's a traumatic thing for them, and it generally takes a broker six months to a year to really get the feel of Century 21. At that point, he understands that he's still his own man, he's still an entrepreneur, and he still runs his own business. He's seen that we don't come in and constantly interfere with his operation. In the end, our brokers are absolutely thrilled with Century 21."

The track record of Century 21 brokers has been outstanding. The concept has proven its worth as the franchisees have experienced continued growth. "The average office has grown dramatically," Art stresses. "The very few who have left Century 21 are those who simply would not follow the system. They just wouldn't use the program, and weren't geared for growth. Since a franchise usually increases substantially in value, many have been sold at large profits. The *new* individual most often follows our system and in turn realizes a huge increase in sales volume."

Today, Art estimates, 80 percent of new franchises are sold to people who approach Century 21, and many more are turned down than are accepted. "When we first got started," he confesses, "we'd take practically anybody. But today we're highly selective. We want the best real estate firm in an area, and we base our selection on business experience, office location, financial stability, and a good reputation in the community."

Many Century 21 brokers have become close friends through conventions and meetings held throughout the year. This network helps operate the VIP referral system. "Each office has a roster of all Century 21 offices," Art explains. "And, you can bet that when a broker in Denver sells the home of a family moving to Chicago, he'll make sure they contact his buddy up there. If he doesn't know anyone in Chicago, he'll go down the roster and pick out somebody in the general area to refer his seller to. This kind of referral system works out very nicely, because both the Denver and the Chicago broker will realize additional commissions."

With a look of satisfaction, he adds, "Do you know that we're probably running over 15,000 referrals a month in Century 21 today from our VIP referral service! Surveys show that about 50 percent of the people who purchased homes in recent years did so more than 50 miles from their previous residences. Furthermore, the average length of tenancy for a family in a given home is only seven years, less than that in some parts of the country.

"I'll repeat what I said earlier. Real estate is big business, getting bigger every day. The big get bigger and the small get smaller. I think that's a fact of the free enterprise system. The big get bigger because they're good and they're offering a lot to the consumer. And as they continue to get bigger, if they're smart, they continue to offer more and more. I think the public recognizes this fact, and when an individual begins to look for a new home, that familiar Century 21 sign and our inter-office referral system become significant factors in his decision to select one of our offices. This is particularly important when people are relocating to an unfamiliar faraway community."

Art points out that Century 21 is a strong believer in taking advantage of the synergistic principle of a franchise system, whereby the total effect is greater than the sum of its parts. Likewise, a planned effort has been made to give Century 21 offices a distinct identity which the public readily recognizes. For instance, there are gold and brown signs prominently displayed in the front of all offices. Equally distinctive Century 21 FOR SALE and SOLD signs are placed in front of homes. Gold Century 21 blazers are worn by both men and women. And with a printing of more than 10 million business cards a month, Century 21 is reported to be the world's largest consumer of business cards.

Although all company printing is done by outside contractors, Century 21 has an art department and a communications department to monitor the quality of the printed sales tools distributed to its brokers and sales representatives. A constant effort is made to provide the best service and delivery of all goods shipped from the Irvine facilities.

Century 21 is continually seeking new methods by which it can service its brokers and sales representatives. It is undoubtedly true that the multicolored printed materials, professionally produced tape cassettes, audio-visual aids, sales aids, and advertising specialty aids that it supplies to franchisees would not be available to an independent broker. "In addition to our national advertising program, and our ongoing communications with our brokers," Art notes, "we're providing the local broker with materials which would be impossible for him to produce on a small scale. For example, we have our two-and-one training program for the new recruit, which is designed for him to take two listings and make one sale. It's an audio-visual teaching program to be used either in-office or in a large training room. Instructor's material is also included so the broker will know how to give the course.

"There are three teaching methods used by the instructor: written material, tape cassettes, and movies. A daily homework assignment for the student is also included. The program is broken down into courses on various facets of the real estate business. It teaches how to list a property, and it's even broken down into specific facets, including canvassing, setting up an appointment, and the close. Each individual segment is covered in a movie. And the movie will automatically stop for an open class discussion, and then it continues to play again. It's utterly fantastic!

"Another wonderful tool we provide for our people," Art adds enthusiastically, "is a twelve-part movie titled *Why List with Century 21?* This is a $100,000 production which we had made by Universal Studios, and it's shown right in the home with a little technicolor showcase. The agent will go into a flip-chart presentation from the film. And yes, we also have all the standard fact-finding and appraisal materials and so forth. There's no way a local broker could afford to equip his sales force with the quality materials we furnish. These materials are the very finest ever to be available in the entire history of the real estate industry."

Art pauses briefly to collect his thoughts. "Another exciting service we're now offering," he continues, "is our International Property Data Bank. While there are good local multiple-listing programs for residential properties, there was never anything offered on a national basis for investment properties. We realize that somewhere between 7 to 10 percent of our sales are in this area. For the first time ever, we're providing our people with a computerized national multiple-listing service for investment properties. For instance, an investor might live in San Diego, but now he can choose investment property to meet his needs from anywhere in the country. With the right return, tax shelter advantages, and who knows what, that property might be somewhere in Columbus, Ohio!"

Another innovative concept of Century 21 is its new relocation centers presently being opened throughout North America. Through a major advertising campaign, as well as through brokers' referrals, prospective home buyers are invited to these relocation centers to be educated about the local community. At these centers they receive an audio-visual presentation on the advantages and drawbacks of the entire metropolitan area. Since a typical broker in a large city doesn't service the entire metropolitan area, he isn't personally in a position to tell the complete story like this. Following the audio-visual presentation, an overlay system placed over a large map displays information for various areas, such as the freeway traffic, giving times and distance of travel during various times of day, smog belt details, recreational facilities, locations of churches and shopping centers, price ranges of homes, flood problems, earthquake problems, and other pertinent facts. Within half an hour the client can zero in on a general area where he would like to live. At that point, the relocation center puts him in touch with a Century 21 broker in that particular community. It's an exciting program which can save months of house-hunting time. Century 21 expects to eventually open fifty relocation centers, each representing about a $50,000 investment.

Recently Century 21 has initiated a home warranty program which is being underwritten by Pacific Cal West, one of the largest warranty companies in North America. Purchasers of resale homes are now covered for any malfunctions during the first year of home ownership for the entire electrical system, the central heating and air-conditioning system, major appliances, the hot water heater, plumbing and drain lines, and heating sheet-metal duct work. The coverage has a small deductible provision to eliminate minor claims.

What else is on the Century 21 drawing board? Art claims that peripheral services such as mortgages, insurance, corporate relocation, moving and storage, title insurance, and home improvement are being discussed. "We're continually looking into many exciting new possibilities," he states. "And the first things we must consider with any idea are: How does it help our brokers and sales representatives? How does it benefit our regions? And, how does it help the consumer?"

A warm smile flashes on his face. "We're a people company. And everybody associated with Century 21 must be people-oriented. This is always foremost on our minds, and it affects everything we do. And that's the way it has to always be."

With that kind of attitude, Century 21 will continue to expand, and as Art puts it, "The big get bigger . . ."

8

Ernest W. Hahn

(ERNEST W. HAHN, INC.)

Ernest Hahn is the founder, chairman of the board, and chief executive officer of Ernest W. Hahn, Inc., one of the largest commercial builders and shopping center developers in America. Headquartered in El Segundo, California, the company has developed thirty-five regional shopping centers with more than 27 million square feet of total retail area. These centers are located throughout California and in Washington, New Mexico, Utah, Colorado, Iowa, Texas, Oregon, and Virginia. An additional thirty shopping centers are planned or under construction throughout the nation, more than any other developer's in North America. In addition, the company has built and/or developed more than 100 ten- to twenty-acre convenience and community centers in California, Nevada, and Washington.

The company began in 1946 as a small general contracting firm and went public in 1972. Wholly owned subsidiaries include Hahn Devcorp, a developer of community and neighborhood shopping centers, and Hahn Property Management Corporation, based in San Diego, a shopping center management firm which handles the management, marketing, security, and maintenance duties for Hahn properties and other developers. For the fiscal year ending February 1979, the company's consolidated statements reported assets of $521 million and revenues in excess of $140 million.

In 1976, Ernest W. Hahn, Inc., was named "best developer" by *Shopping Center World Magazine.* Ernie is the past president of the International Council of Shopping Centers, a 9,000-member international trade association, and has been active in Associated General Contractors and numerous other civic and trade groups. He is a founding trustee and donor of the Eisenhower Medical Center and Hospital at Palm Springs, California; a trustee of Scripps Clinic and Research Foundation, La Jolla, California; and a trustee of the Independent Colleges of Southern California. He is a leading supporter of Centinela Valley Community Hospital, Children's Hospital of Los Angeles, and the Los Angeles and Centinela Valley YMCA's. He sponsors the Ernest W. Hahn Fellowship at City of Hope, and is a former recipient of the Golden Torch of Hope. In October 1977, Ernie was inducted into the Leuzinger High School Hall of Fame in Hawthorne, California.

He has been honored for these activities and for his "general contributions to the cause of brotherhood and racial and religious understanding in his industry and the general community" by the Real Estate and Construction Industries Division of the National Conference of Christians and Jews. He is also a recipient of the Golden Plate Award of the American Academy of Achievement, a national organization dedicated to the advancement of youth and education.

In May, 1977, the Ernest W. Hahn Award was established at the Harvard Business School. The award supports significant academic contributions "to the development, improvement and evolution of regional shopping centers or such other alternate facilities as may exist to provide the most efficient distribution of goods and services to the public." It also recognizes "the enrichment of environmental, cultural and recreational aspects of such forms of distribution."

Born in New York City on September 12, 1919, Ernie was raised and educated in the Los Angeles–South Bay area. He served in the U.S. Navy as an enlisted man. In 1946, after leaving Northrop Aircraft, Inc., where he had been an executive, he co-founded the Hahn–St. John construction firm. Hahn–St. John became Ernest W. Hahn, Inc., in 1956.

His hobbies include tennis, golf, fishing, hunting, and flying. In 1974, his winery, Chateau Montelena in Napa, California, won the Chardonnay wine award. He and his wife, Jean, live in Indian Wells, California, and he daily flies his own airplane to his El Segundo office. The Hahns have three children—Ronald, Charlene, and Christine—and seven grandchildren.

Ernie Hahn entered the construction business in 1946 with an old high school buddy. "We started a small general contracting business which specialized in remodeling and small commercial jobs in Hawthorne, California," he says with a broad smile. "Our first office was in the corner of a used furniture store. We had no money for rent and no furniture. We started out doing storefront remodeling, and our first full job was a $7,000 commercial building in Inglewood. At the time, that was a big job for us. Since my partner was a carpenter, he did the outside work, and I took care of the office estimating and the selling."

During the prosperous postwar years the Hahn–St. John Construction Company grew rapidly. Ernie says the firm was busy right from the start, and before long the partners were doing two jobs, then three jobs, and soon as many as fifteen or twenty jobs at a time. Soon they put up a 1,200-square-foot office building across the street from their furniture store/office building. By the early 1950s, they were building as many as 700 to 800 houses each year. At that time they made a decision to specialize in industrial and commercial construction. The two young entrepreneurs obtained most of their work in the Hawthorne area, where they had grown up, and as the business community expanded, so did the Hahn–St. John Construction Company.

By 1956, the company was doing in excess of $100 million each year in constructing stores, industrial buildings, schools, and shopping centers. Although the two partners had worked very successfully together, Ernie's partner, Stewart St. John, decided that he wanted to specialize in government contracting, while Ernie wanted to concentrate in commercial work. At this point, Ernie bought out St. John, and Ernest W. Hahn, Inc., was established.

Ernie's background was appropriate for construction management. For a short time after graduating from high school, he worked as a teller at the Bank of America. During this period, he studied financial courses and real estate. In 1940, having become friendly with Jack Northrop by cashing his checks at the bank, he accepted an offer to work for Northrop Aircraft in cost estimating. The aircraft company, which has 20,000 employees today, at this time had a staff of only thirty-nine. At Northrop, he moved into industrial engineering and took some management courses at UCLA and USC. Northrop also sent Ernie to Detroit, where he studied mass production methods applicable to the aircraft industry.

"I believe my background at Northrop was very useful in my construction career," Ernie states. "Our big forte was cost control. And without question this was the strong suit which got us work in our early days. The postwar years were fairly inflationary, and people would start plans never knowing what their costs were going to be. We sold them on our cost-control approach.

"Once the plans are drawn, there's no such thing as cost control," the shopping center executive states emphatically, "and that was our whole sales pitch. Cost control must be exercised in the architectural stages. We could give them a firm price early in the game, providing we had some latitude with their architect. We didn't request the right to change design,

ERNEST W. HAHN

but we did want to be able to control the cost by ingenious structural methods or substitution of acceptable materials.

"Instead of bidding on an endless number of jobs where we had no control over cost, we devoted our efforts to controlling the cost of a project during the planning stages. Seventy-five percent of the development dollar is the construction cost and the architectural and engineering fees associated with it. If we can save 10 percent by being diligent in cost control, we'll pick up 7½ percent in the total cost of the project. That's substantial. And that's where we have always concentrated our efforts."

He goes on in a more serious tone, "Today's inflationary economy offers opportunities like those of the postwar period. This is a perfect time to capitalize on performing a cost-saving service. The most difficult time to be in this business, on the other hand, is during a downswing in the economy. That's where you're going to find many contractors sitting around with no work and willing to bid on anything just to keep their organizations intact. They're willing to work for nothing just to keep their equipment busy. Because there's so little building going on, many contractors compete for the same jobs, and drive the price structure down. In an inflationary period, however, a developer can compete by taking the risk out of a project for his client at an early stage of the game where he can modify, reshape, and rethink the program on the basis of firm costs. I believe this is of paramount importance.

"The second thing after cost saving is to build the project in a shorter period of time," Ernie stresses. "This not only saves interest, but it gets the client into business early. This is extremely important to a retailer. With a manufacturing facility, there's a long start-up period, placement of equipment, and so on after the building is up, so the time element isn't normally nearly as important. But a retailer? He's ready to go at it! He's aiming for two seasons, before Christmas and early spring before Easter. These seasons are absolutely critical. That's why scheduled accomplishment is mandatory in this business.

"It can sometimes be a problem when a major department store is ready to move into a center but no other tenants are available at that time," he says with a frown. "The major may think the area is so good that he's willing to open free-standing for six months to a year. Our problem is $20 million worth of bricks and mortar sitting out there with no revenue coming in—just because the major opens up! His opening complicates matters, because now we have to burn the lights at night and maintain the parking lot. Our whole economic base changes the day he opens. If we don't put tenants in the center, the pressure is really on us!

"From a practical point of view, very few major stores want to be in a mall without other tenants. But on occasion it happens that a major has a tough schedule, opening so many stores within a given year, and wants to space out its administrative load. Bon Marche, for instance, is known to do that up North, where it has a tremendous schedule."

Ernest W. Hahn, Inc., grew to become one of the largest contractors in the United States specializing in retail construction. In some years, its construction volume is as high as $140 million. Today the company's contracting division has a $250 million backlog. During the late 1950s, Ernie made the decision also to develop the company's own properties. "It was logical that we should become developers," the trim suntanned Californian explains, "because we could really control the costs then. And the relationship we had developed with the retail chains and drug chains made it a natural for us to think about doing our own centers.

"But our biggest motivation was the fact that we'd been in the business for about fifteen years, and even with our large construction volume, our net worth was only about $400,000. We didn't have the development profits, and we just weren't retaining very much after paying our corporate taxes each year. Once we began to develop, our equity built up dramatically. Based on the present market value of our holdings, our equities are about $250 million."

The company built its first regional shopping center about

fifteen years ago in Santa Barbara. "A regional shopping center," Ernie explains, "has two or more department stores and many mall stores. At that time, most of the centers we built were open malls. Subsequently we went to closed ones, but in certain select locations we'll still construct open malls."

A look of satisfaction appears on his face. "Prior to completing the Santa Barbara center, we took the gamble of a lifetime. In Montclair, which is out toward San Bernardino, we bought some ground for $340,000. That was an amount nearly equal to our entire net worth! We undertook to build a closed-mall regional center with Broadway Stores, the May Company, and J. C. Penney. It was a very big step for us and we deliberated about it for a long time. However, it turned out to be so successful that even before it was completed we branched out into another one. As a result, we became highly involved in regionals. We established a relationship with such major department stores in this area as the Broadway, J. C. Penney, and Sears. Soon we were averaging two or three regionals a year, with the majority of our development, until recently, in the metropolitan Los Angeles area. Today we have thirty regionals in the planning stage, ten of those under construction."

Ernie insists that a regional shopping center cannot be built without the inclusion of major department stores. "It takes two or more majors," he asserts, "and then we're in business. Smaller stores know that the public recognizes the majors because they do a tremendous amount of advertising. They're selling nationally made products, and due to their mass purchasing and mass merchandising, they're allotted a tremendous amount of national and local advertising dollars by the manufacturer. Those advertising dollars may create ten to twelve pages daily of ads for stores like the Broadway or May Company. Of course, that's what brings people to the regionals. Historically, throughout the world, the department store has always been the 'bell cow.'"

"Bell cow" is a term used frequently in the shopping center

industry. It refers to the lead department store (lead cow) which a developer may plan an entire shopping center around. Once the bell cow store is signed up, it draws other tenants. The majors know this. "We just break even on most of our dealings with the bell cow store," Ernie states matter-of-factly. "In some cases we even subsidize them. For instance, we may give them free ground if they come in quickly. That enables us to establish our center, so that major is what we call a 'pivotal store.' It may be Foley's in Texas, or Bamberger's in New Jersey, or perhaps Neiman-Marcus, or Sears, or Bon Marche. We don't expect to break even on those stores. We might give them the ten acres necessary to build their store, and their share of the parking lot. The majors will own their building, so in most cases we end up owning only the stores in the mall and the ground supporting it, such as the parking lot and building passage. In effect, we end up being co-developers with the majors.

"Although the majors build and own their own buildings, they'll normally pay their share of the maintenance, taxes, and certain expenses, such as a contribution yearly toward the operation of the closed mall. Our leasing income is based on a percentage of the gross sales volume of mall stores, but we derive no net income from the majors."

To someone unfamiliar with a regional shopping center's practices, it may appear that the smaller mall stores operate under less favorable conditions. They pay high rents, and in addition they pay a percentage of their gross sales to the developer. But Ernie explains, "There's an amazing number of tenants who want to be located in regional malls and advertise seeking spaces. They know their volume will be anywhere from three to ten times as much in a regional center. They also know that rent is the retailer's least significant cost. The biggest expense is the payroll. When you're doing volume, rent is nothing. Absolutely nothing!"

Ernie goes on to outline factors he considers in signing up tenants for a mall, since one of the keys to success in a regional shopping center is the right mix of tenants. "The biggest thing we look for," he says, "is the proper allocation of space with the right type of merchandise. And, of course, at the right location within the center. We're interested in utilizing our space in a way that benefits our tenants. It's important to get the proper balance so everybody will profit. You wouldn't want to have a shopping center that was all shoe stores or all women's stores. The retailers come into a center because they want to be part of a synergistic, well-balanced group of stores which are joining together to do the best possible job."

It is commonly believed that major department stores are in a position to dictate which retailers will be included in a shopping center. The Reciprocal Easement Agreement (REA), the bible of all shopping center developers, which is carefully scrutinized by the FTC (Fair Trade Commission), clearly specifies that a department store may not exercise any undue pressure to discourage competition. "Of course, the REA gives certain rights to the department store," Ernie states. "For example, a major can have the right to determine what kind of store leases space within a certain distance from their door, say 100 or 150 feet. They might not want, for instance, all fast-food restaurants surrounding their main entrance. They can also specify that a certain percentage of that hundred feet be no more than 7 percent food or 6 percent better women's wear, or whatever it is, depending, of course, on the tenants. They can't keep out a specific retailer, however, nor can they dictate in what space a tenant should be located. Their rights are carefully defined. Since they're making a ten- to twelve-million-dollar commitment to the center in capital expenditures, I don't think those terms are unreasonable."

Leases are drawn up with the mall stores for a fixed rent plus a percentage of the retailer's sales volume. As inflation pushes up the price of merchandise in the stores and total sales revenues increase, the rental income also rises. Because of this trend, shopping centers have proven to be inflation-proof investments for developers. This is especially true with today's long-term leases, which have standard provisions stating that the mall tenants must pay their pro rata share of taxes and maintenance costs. Ernie illustrates: "Let's take an example of a center with a minimum rent income of $4 million in which we have zero equity because we have 100 percent financing from the insurance company. And, incidentally, that's a typical loan on a regional center. After servicing our debt and paying our expenses, let's say that we're generating a 10 percent cash flow, or $400,000. If the following year there's a 10 percent inflationary factor, it's going to be reflected in the revenues of all sales in the mall. So theoretically our revenues will increase to $4.4 million. That $400,000 above the $4 million is not required to service the debt, which is constant. Whatever the taxes and maintenance cost, the tenants are paying them, so we're going to realize an additional $400,000. Of course, if a store doesn't generate its minimum, which can happen during an inflationary trend, then there's not going to be any overage rent from that tenant. At some point in time, however, over a period of years, they all get to their minimum, and then those inflationary dollars represent a 100 percent return to the overage rent revenues."

In a lower voice Ernie adds, "A recession can hurt us, but when the sales volume drops, we still get the minimum rents. That's not a crisis, because when we build, our projections are based on these amounts being an adequate return. However, if we get a terrible recession and the stores can't operate profitably, the center ends up with vacant stores—and that would hurt badly. This hasn't happened yet, even with all the recessions we've experienced. We've had only twelve turnovers in twenty centers during the '73–'74 recession. Our present vacancy in all of our centers is less than 1 percent."

This successful track record indicates that Ernie's malls are well placed. He acknowledges that major department stores are his company's greatest source of leads in determining the site of a new regional shopping center. "The majors are in a continual expansion program," he asserts, "and they have a tremendous amount of ongoing research, so that they're high-ly informed on the demographics and economic base of an area. Frequently they approach us, naming an area where they'd like to open a store. We then do computer runs our-selves on population growth factors, using computer services. Coldwell Banker, to name one such service, has a new com-puter facility which we're building for them right across the street from us, and which can provide a developer with census tracts and demographic information on practically any area in the United States. So we'll reinforce the department store's research to satisfy ourselves that a regional is viable. General-ly, when we have two, three, or four department stores who concur on an area based on their research, we're pretty darn sure."

The reason Ernest W. Hahn, Inc., is today in the enviable position of having department stores approach the company is that, as Ernie puts it, "We have established a good relation-ship with all of the major chains, and *they feel comfortable with us.* They know they're going to get a quality product, and they know we're financially responsible. In California and the Far West states, we've become the dominant developer, and that's a reputation we've worked diligently to earn. I know that in other parts of the country certain other firms enjoy the same recognition. There are probably about fifteen developers throughout the country who are readily accepted by the chains, and the fifteen of us develop about 90 percent of all re-gional shopping center space in the United States. Basically, each one has a sphere of influence, a particular geographic area. Of course, that doesn't mean that my firm won't build anywhere in the United States and other developers won't come into our area. There's nothing cut and dried about it. We have gradually grown out of our original sphere of influ-ence and started leapfrogging around the country."

Today, Ernest W. Hahn, Inc., has regional shopping centers located as far east as Hampton, Virginia, and a major mall scheduled to open in Memphis, Tennessee, in late 1980.

Bridgewater Commons in Bridgewater, New Jersey, is scheduled to open in fall 1982, as is Woodbridge Mall in Woodbridge, Virginia, just outside Washington, D.C.

Ernie takes great pride in each Hahn property, but is especially enthusiastic about the Woodbridge Mall. He points out that it will contain 1.1 million square feet of proposed retail area, and that four of its six proposed majors are Woodward & Lathrop, Sears, J. C. Penney, and Hecht's.

"Woodbridge will be about twenty miles south of downtown Washington," Ernie says. "The area is growing very rapidly, so we're putting in six department stores. We believe that the Woodbridge Mall will become the focal point of everything in that whole community. Right now, it's basically a rural area with nothing much but gas stations, small stores, and a whole lot of houses being built. And nobody today is building new cities in areas like this. So with the continuation of suburban growth in this northern Virginia area, our mall will be the town center. The Woodbridge Mall will have a town square. The shops will include a farmers' market, a gourmet butcher, several gourmet fruit and vegetable stands, and a tobacconist's. There will be banks and a savings and loan, and three car showrooms, each of them large enough to show two or three automobiles. We'll have an ice-skating rink with terrace restaurants, and a theater square with sit-down restaurants and a theater, so people can go out to dine and then to the theater. The development will also contain several acres of beautiful parks. We're using colonial architecture borrowed from Alexandria and Williamsburg. The outside landscaping will be breathtaking, and we'll have park-and-ride facilities so a shopper can park his car and pick up the transit into the capital."

Ernie believes that people go to regional shopping centers for several reasons. In addition to the comparative shopping, convenient parking, and wide selections of merchandise, the malls create an aura of excitement. "To some people," he remarks with a smile, "the mall is a place to sit and watch people. It's a gathering spot, an elongated town square!"

An outstanding feature of both existing properties and proposed malls is that *each center looks different.* "We don't build the traditional cookie-cutter centers of the 'sixties," Ernie stresses. "We have never put up two centers that look the same. Each center is tailored to the area it's located in. Perhaps it's more expensive to build this way, but we think it's more productive, because we can put in architectural amenities and services catering to that particular community."

To illustrate the contrasting themes and decor of Hahn shopping centers, Ernie focuses on University Towne Centre in San Diego. He beams with obvious pride. This center has 889,000 square feet of total retail area with three major stores (the Broadway, Robinson's, and Sears) and 126 shops and boutiques. Adjacent residential units include eighty condominiums, forty single-family residences, and sixty apartments. In addition, the open-air mall includes an Olympic-size Ice Capades skating rink, a preschool, an international folk art museum with an adjacent preserved natural canyon, and a bicycle path. There is a six-screen movie theater, a 350-seat public auditorium, conference facilities for the University of San Diego's adult education classes, dance classrooms, six community meeting rooms, an artisan's gallery, a discotheque-restaurant; the list could go on and on. "It has 50,000 square feet of non-revenue-producing space," Ernie points out, "and this center still has the greatest cash flow per square foot *after* supporting the non-revenue-producing space of any center we have."

Approximately 1,300 people are employed in University Towne Centre's stores and other facilities, with that figure approaching 2,000 during the holiday seasons. It is estimated that an average of 25,000 people per day visit the center. In May 1978, University Towne Centre received an award from the International Council of Shopping Centers for its outstanding contribution to the shopping center industry. The national award recognized the company's achievement in developing the multiple-use complex. San Diego's mayor, Pete Wilson, stated, "The Towne Centre is the kind of 'people place' that naturally belongs in San Diego. I am convinced it will serve as a model for future development in this city."

"I think the mayor's description of University Towne Centre is right in line with our philosophy," Ernie remarks. "We make people feel comfortable there, and that makes them want to patronize it. We put a lot of thought into making people comfortable in our centers. We give our architect four pages of criteria which help integrate our center into the community. We believe that it's a company's responsibility to soften the blow of a new center which is going to produce a great deal of traffic and masses of people in one place; we don't want to have a harsh impact on the community. So even though we may have a large center, it won't be overwhelming. In some cities, for example, we'll exceed the landscaping requirements by two and three times. We're careful to avoid high light standards; we'll use low standards to keep the glare from the neighborhoods. And we're not required to do that. That's our criterion.

"We'll never have artificial flowers. We shy away from fountains and water because they're difficult to maintain properly and they tend to become unsightly 'attractive nuisances.' We'd rather put the money into good art. We may commission well-known artists for a particular mall because we think that's a far better way of doing things than putting in gurgling fountains which aren't functional and can't be maintained. And we don't believe in merchandising in the mall. We don't have a single center which has a kiosk inside, nor are any of the public areas used to sell anything. We believe that people ought to have a place to relax, and shouldn't be annoyed by merchants peddling costume jewelry, glasses, tea rings, or other small things in the center of the public spaces. If there's a need for that kind of merchandise, it can just as well be placed at the sides of the mall in normal retailing areas.

"The public place is for the public, and not just during regular shopping center hours," he declares. "We make it available for the community's use. Last year in Hawthorne, for instance, two high schools wanted to have a joint homecoming dance, with the Harry James orchestra. They'd wanted to do this for years, but could never find a place large enough. We invited them to use the mall, and for the first time they were able to do something together. And they didn't have to pay any money to rent a hall. Everybody told us, 'You're going to have problems with the kids.' The truth of the matter is that we didn't have any security problems whatsoever. Nothing was disturbed. Absolutely no vandalism, not a single flower touched. The whole secret is *It's their center.* And they have high regard for it."

Ernie looks serious. "I'm getting philosophical now," he says. "The Hawthorne Plaza, located in an area which is about 50 percent minorities, is a good example of community responsibility. While many developers shy away from this kind of area, we went ahead and built it, knowing that the trade area contained many black, Oriental, and Spanish people. We felt that people in the community would think, Here's a developer who came in and did this for our community. He's going to make a profit, obviously. Still, he came in and did this after we were here! Other mall owners try to get out of these areas. But we put beautiful flowers and landscaping throughout the center. There are bridges going to the mall from the parking area, and these bridges and stairways overflow with flowers and planters. We did the same thing in the alleyways behind the center.

"Why should we have a center in a minority area with these added touches? Because I don't care whether you're black or green, you have a love for living things, and you're going to appreciate them. And the result of our faith in the community is that we have fewer security problems at Hawthorne than at some centers in more affluent areas. Those are *their* flowers. And it's profitable for us to do it this way!

"We build what the people want and like instead of what the developer wants and likes. Too often, the developer is merely expressing *his* desires instead of the people's. Some of our competitors seem to feel that magnificent statements are the important thing. We believe in more lasting things. The old plazas, the old towns, and the old streets in Paris and Madrid are still nice places to shop. We like that sort of thing. So our storefronts in our new centers are three feet out beyond the structural walls. Because we're charging the tenant for the additional space, he naturally designs his store to take advantage of that particular space. When the tenant moves his storefront out, it becomes three-dimensional because there are three-foot separations between all storefronts, and suddenly our malls look like little Paris streets. When a person is walking through the mall, he can see the merchandise from the side and not just the front. It no longer looks like a bunch of movie sets with signs over the top. It's now become a street!

"That's the direction of our approach today," Ernie explains. "We want people to feel like they're in a little Paris street, a street in Williamsburg or Alexandria, not a toothpaste-tube tunnel with air conditioning. We want them to feel comfortable so they'll stay there. Let them walk up one side of the mall, and then back down the other side. If they see things, then they'll impulsively buy them. Our statistics indicate that *43 percent of all purchasing is impulse buying.* But in order for people to get impulsive, they have to be exposed to the merchandise, and they have to be there long enough to get that exposure."

Ernie also notes that because he picks an architectural style which has lasted for a hundred years or more in the community, it isn't necessary to remodel a center every few years or so. "If you chose the chrome and glass-block style of the 'fifties, you'd have to redo it in seven years." He chuckles. "We want people to be comfortable, so our centers are more in keeping with what's around them in the whole area and, as a result, will be compatible for decades.

"We also build our centers so they'll introduce as much sunlight, sky, and outside as possible in suitable climatic conditions. Flowers and trees are universal. Everybody loves them! Who hates a tree? Who hates plants? Our centers have two- and three-story-high specimen trees and we don't gimmick them up. We try, too, to use comfortable, warm materials."

Ernie leans back in his chair in a relaxed manner. "The people don't view us as that 'big ugly developer who built that monolithic hideous structure,'" he says with deserved satisfaction.

He recalls one particular instance in San Diego, when he was addressing a crowd of young people in the mall. "I don't normally like to be in crowds and identified as the developer, particularly with young people, who aren't impressed with big business. However, I was introduced and received tremendous applause. I thought that it was just polite, but then a few people from the audience started to spontaneously yell, 'We love your center.' 'Thanks for University Towne Centre.' I just can't tell you how rewarding that was to me."

9

Samuel J. LeFrak

(LEFRAK ORGANIZATION, INC.)

Samuel J. LeFrak is the chairman of the board of Lefrak Organization, Inc., a Forest Hills, New York, building and development company recognized as one of the largest in the world.

Lefrak Organization is engaged in the creation of commercial, industrial, and residential projects. The company is also one of the world's largest construction-management firms and has major interests in community planning, mortgage financing, and financial investments.

Sam was elected president of the family-owned corporation in 1948, and became chairman of the board in 1975, the same year that his son, Richard, was named president. Sam succeeded his father, Harry, who as a young immigrant had founded the business in 1905, when he invested his entire capital in the construction of one single-family home in Brooklyn. Recognizing the need for residential construction, Harry soon began to build entire blocks of private homes in Brooklyn. Sam grew up in the building business, and at the young age of eight he began to work with his father in construction. Under his leadership, Lefrak Organization has become one of the world's greatest building companies. The annual revenue of the privately held company is believed to be in the hundreds of millions of dollars.

The Lefrak Organization is presently the major force in Battery Park City, the nation's largest urban development, which is scheduled to be completed in the early 1980s. The company also owns and operates major office buildings and industrial properties throughout the United States. One such prime office building is the Squibb Building, a 700,000-square-foot structure at 40 West 57th Street in Manhattan.

Major non–real estate investments include Lefrak Oil & Gas Organization (LOGO) founded in Tulsa, Oklahoma, in 1971, which quickly became one of the fastest-growing independent oil and gas companies in Oklahoma. In 1978, the company invested an estimated $10 million in twenty-two exploratory and twenty-eight development prospects. In 1975, Sam also founded The Entertainment Company, a music publishing/record production firm. The company's annual volume is estimated to exceed $10 million. It has recorded such superstars as Barbra Streisand, Glen Campbell, Dolly Parton, Helen Reddy, and Cheryl Ladd. Another family enterprise, Lefrak Productions, a film company with headquarters in Los Angeles, is headed by Sam's daughter Francine.

Civic activities have long occupied a major portion of Sam's time. In 1957, he was chairman of the National Conference of Christians and Jews Brotherhood Night. He was commissioner of the Public Works Borough of Manhattan in 1958 and also a member of the Greater New York Safety Council's Advisory Committee. He has served on the advisory board of the Chemical Bank. In 1960, he was appointed overseas adviser to the State of Israel. During the same year, he was elected trustee of the Citizens Budget Commission, Inc., named a member of the Manhattan, Queens, and Brooklyn real estate boards, and elected a trustee of the Citizen's Housing and Planning Council of New York, Inc.

In 1963–64, Sam visited Thailand and, at the request of its ruler, studied and reported on the government's housing. In 1963, he was appointed to the Advisory Committee of U.S. Government Housing, and to the Committee on World Housing of the United Nations. He was a director of the New York World's Fair in 1964–65. In 1966, he served on Governor Rockefeller's Finance and Advisory Committee of State Traffic Safety Council, and he was also elected commissioner of the Landmarks Preservation Commission of New York City. The following year, he was a United States delegate to the International Conference for Housing and Urban Development in Switzerland and was also elected president of the New York City Commercial Development Corporation. In 1968, he was elected a board member of the Sales Executive Club of New York and a board member of the U.S.O. He was appointed a special consultant for urban affairs by the State Department in 1969, and the same year he became a United States delegate to the Economic Commission for Europe on air pollution.

In 1970, he became a member of the advisory board of the Real Estate Institute of New York University and a founding member of the World Business Council. In 1971, Sam was named a member of the board of trustees at New York Law School and was a guest lecturer at Harvard University's Graduate School of Business Administration. In 1972, he was appointed a member of the board of governors of the Invest in America National Council and named a director of the Consumer Credit Counseling Service of New York. In 1974, he was a member of Mayor Beame's Committee on Housing Development, and of the executive board of the Greater New York Councils for the Boy Scouts of America. He also served on Governor Carey's Task Force on Housing. In 1975, he was a guest lecturer at Yale University and a featured speaker at the Institutional Investor Real Estate Conference. In the same year he was elected to the board of directors of the Lotos Club, the New York City Industrial Development Corporation, and the Executive Committee of the Citizens Committee of New York City, Inc.

In 1977, he was a guest speaker at New York University and a board member of the New York City Convention and Exhibition Center Corporation. In 1978, he was named a member of the American Jewish Congress and a board member of the Friars Foundation. He lectured at Pace University and was reappointed for a third time to a six-year term by Governor Hugh Carey as a commissioner in the Saratoga–Capitol District State Park and Recreation Commission.

His philanthropic activities are too numerous to list. One major endeavor is the LeFrak Foundation, founded by Sam in 1953, which has since disbursed millions of dollars for all phases of social work without regard to race, color, or creed. Sam has also served in many capacities for the Federation of Jewish Philanthropies. The Samuel J. LeFrak Library was dedicated at the University of Maryland in 1960. He is president of the Samuel J. and Ethel LeFrak Foundation, and was president of the Harry and Sarah LeFrak Foundation, Inc. He was honored by Pope John XXIII and decorated with the Order of St. John of Jerusalem. Sam has served on many hospital boards. He is a patron of the New York Philharmonic, a sponsor of the Metropolitan Opera, and a sponsor of the City Center of Music and Drama.

Numerous honors have been bestowed upon Sam. A few of these awards are: a medal for Outstanding Community Service for New York in 1962; the World's Fair Silver Medallion in 1964–65; the John F. Kennedy Peace Award in 1966; the Master Builder Award by the New York Cardiac Center in 1968; the Builder of Excellence Award from Brandeis University; the Distinguished Alumnus Award by the University of Maryland Alumni Association in 1970; the Award of Merit by the Lotos Club in 1973; the Fifth Avenue Association Architectural Award, and the Queens Chamber of Commerce Award for Excellence in Design in 1974.

A graduate of the University of Maryland, Sam attended the Graduate School of Finance at Columbia University and the Graduate School of Business Administration at Harvard University. He has several honorary degrees, including doctor of science, London College of Applied Science, England; consulate laureate, University of Studies, Rome; doctor of laws, New York Law School; and doctor of laws, Colgate University.

Sam was born in Manhattan on February 12, 1918. He and his wife, Ethel, have four children—Denise, Richard, Francine, and Jacqueline. They live in New York City.

It's natural to associate the name Sam LeFrak with apartment buildings. His firm, Lefrak Organization, Inc., is the nation's largest landlord of apartment buildings, and certainly dominates the New York City market. *One out of sixteen New Yorkers lives in a Lefrak apartment!*

However, Sam LeFrak's holdings are not limited to apartment buildings. The Lefrak Organization also owns major office buildings and industrial properties throughout the United States. The dynamic chief executive proudly claims, "We've built everything imaginable—a hydro-electric plant, an airport, a deep-water port, and a large landfill. We've built a city, brick by brick. Our diversified portfolio includes shopping centers, office buildings, industrial parks, *and* housing."

Sam gestures broadly. "You know, land is a raw material," he says authoritatively, "and it presents us with choices. We can drill it. We can mine it. We can use it for agriculture. Or we can develop it. We always look for the highest and best use. Land is only as good as the improvement that's placed on it."

A member of the President's National Energy Council, Sam LeFrak obviously practices what he preaches. Lefrak

SAMUEL J. LEFRAK

Organization consists of more than 350 corporations, which not only develop and manage real estate, but also have major commitments in gas and oil exploration, mining and agriculture.

Sam's attitude towards his oil and gas activities clearly illustrates his zeal and enthusiasm for *any* project he is involved in. Since it started in Tulsa, Oklahoma, in early 1971, Lefrak Oil & Gas Organization (LOGO) has drilled wells throughout the central sector of the United States from the Gulf of Mexico to the Canadian border. While the company initially restricted its activities to taking working interests in oil and gas ventures, by 1979 Sam had allocated $50 to $60 million to finance LOGO drilling. He expects the company to double its activities each year and eventually become the most active independent oil company in the country. While that sounds like a bold objective for a newcomer in the petroleum industry, Sam LeFrak has always been a man who *dares to think big.* Perhaps his philosophy is best summed up by a sign in his office which reads, THERE IS NOTHING IMPOSSIBLE. IT JUST HASN'T BEEN DONE BEFORE.

He stresses that the company has no interest in drilling dry holes for tax write-offs. "We're looking for production!" His expression serious, he explains: "There's a tremendous challenge in being in the oil and gas industry. I feel a patriotic responsibility. It reminds me of the victory gardens grown during World War Two to free up food for the defense forces. And, as I said when we got into it, 'What the hell, if we're going to be a consumer and supplies are short, let's go out and find it, drill it up ourselves, and supply ourselves so we can be self-sufficient.'

"Today the Lefrak Organization consumes about 25 million gallons of fuel a year," he continues. "Now, we're producing 4,000 barrels a day from our own oil and gas development operations. So whatever I'm paying to the utility company or the purveyor of heavy oil or the gas station, I'm picking up at the wellhead. With the cost of energy skyrocketing, I have a tremendous leverage factor, don't I?"

Sam moves his arms and hands rapidly as he talks. "We're drilling strictly in the United States. We're not interested in going to the Middle East. It's very important that we develop the oil industry in America. We must have our own sources of energy. I do not intend to spend the rest of my life hat in hand begging some sheik for barrels of oil. And why should we make those Greek tanker owners even richer, as we do when we transport it to this country? That's counterproductive, and it adversely affects the value of the dollar. So we want to find it here!"

In June 1979, the Lefrak Organization drew national attention when Sam declared war on OPEC. The price of fuel oil had risen in one year from thirty-nine cents per gallon to fifty-five cents per gallon. "We're at war," Sam stresses, "an energy war. We can't let the machinations of the OPEC nations destroy our dollar, destroy our economy, destroy our way of life. This is a war we can win and must win." Sam fought back by converting 9,214 Lefrak apartment units from oil to natural gas, the largest such energy conversion ever. More than 6 million gallons of imported fuel oil were saved during the 1979–80 heating season. Although the conversion, with a cost approaching $10 million, resulted in little immediate savings, it is expected to keep costs stable as the OPEC nations continue to escalate the price of oil.

Why the conversion? "My interest is in doing everything possible to create energy independence for the United States," Sam explains. "Gas is America's best hope for the future. It's an American fuel and it's the way to break the chains binding us to foreign oil producers. Unless the United States frees itself from dependency upon foreign oil, we will be subjected to ever-increasing economic blackmail. Oil imports are a major danger to the economy and to our military security. This government and its industries can no longer afford to ignore or downplay the fact that natural gas can fill much of our energy needs, cut foreign oil chains, and sharply reduce the disastrous $50 billion drain to oil-producing countries. Let's come up with American solutions to our energy problems. Now is the time for creativity and determination."

Sam pauses briefly and goes on in his booming voice: "Sure, I'm in business to make a profit, but often I act in the public interest rather than strictly as a businessman. Of course, there are times when the two concerns come together. I think one must look for a balance."

Sam expanded his housing activities in the New York area following World War II, when thousands of returning veterans found themselves living in temporary Quonset huts or other substandard housing. "I thought then," he states, "as I think now, that the very basis of a man's dignity is a reasonable place in which to live and raise his family. I began building then and I have never stopped. My guideline has always been the same: 'Give the people the housing they want at a price they can afford to pay.' "

Lefrak City, a $150 million complex housing 25,000 people is a prime example of Sam's philosophy of providing attractive housing at affordable prices. Lefrak City consists of twenty eighteen-story apartment houses, a total of 5,000 units, located on a forty-acre site just off the Long Island Expressway in Queens. It contains two office buildings, a post office, a library, four schools, a 3,000-car underground garage and a 1,000-car ground level garage, a shopping plaza, a 1,200-seat motion picture theater, swimming pools, tennis courts, squash courts, a health club, and much more. The average rental rate is a highly competitive $65 per room. Many people are employed full-time at Lefrak City. In addition, part-time workers and moonlighters can work evenings to supplement their regular incomes and walk back to their apartments in a few minutes.

Located only fifteen minutes from midtown Manhattan, Lefrak City offers many features of a suburban environment. "We're able to keep the rent down," Sam emphasizes, "because we financed Lefrak City ourselves; we're not paying today's interest rates, which I consider to be usurious. The office and retail space also helps subsidize the housing. We have about 2.5 million square feet of office space and close to a million square feet of retail space. So the income that's generated on the commercial and retail end allows us to offer our apartment units at attractive rents."

Sam's face glows with pride when he talks about Lefrak City, undoubtedly the biggest jewel in the Lefrak Organization's crown. "Lefrak City represents a city within a city. And with this country's energy problems, we need more and more of this kind of 'satellite city.' We need scores of new satellite cities within our major urban areas if these urban areas are to survive. A satellite city like Lefrak City is built on a foundation of existing city services. Remember, Queens had a subway and highways built and paid for before Lefrak City was put up. What we did was use what already existed in a revolutionary way. Today the ecologists call this recycling. We did it before they labeled it.

"The suburbs can no longer sustain an exodus from the city. In the face of dwindling energy supplies, nothing is more wasteful than the suburban one-family home. And what's more energy-saving than a community with housing, schools, business facilities, entertainment, shopping, and churches all available through the most economical form of transportation—walking!

"Another thing about Lefrak City," Sam points out, "it was built with not one cent of public money! I did not ask for and did not receive any tax abatement or tax consideration. On the contrary, the tax assessment is very high. And it is a self-contained community with its own fire, police, and sanitation departments. Since it is a private community without any public streets, it is the owner who has the prime responsibility for health, safety and welfare, not the bureaucracy."

Since it was completed in 1962, Lefrak City has had a crime rate substantially lower than all the surrounding areas. The community represents proof that free enterprise can supply housing for the average American and at the same time stop the flight to the suburbs. Planners throughout the world have studied it and discovered that it works. It has been emulated in London, Rome, and Tokyo.

Sam beams. "Before Lefrak City was built, the forty-acre site it stands on provided New York City with $16,000 in annual taxes. Today we pay approximately $7 million a year in real estate taxes! It's a classic instance of everybody benefiting. Lefrak City is a truly remarkable example of what the free enterprise system can do."

Sam delights in pointing out, "I've done it myself, without the government." He strongly believes that too much political interference has stifled the real estate industry in recent years. "It's so counterproductive," he says with a grim look. "The pressure from the environmentalists, OSHA, and the zoning requirements is overwhelming. The bureaucrats have invaded the industry. There was a time when I enjoyed what I refer to as 'the freedom of the seas,' but today it's one regulation after another. It's very frustrating. We need zoning laws that will let us build affordable housing in our cities. We need revised construction codes that will let us use new materials, new techniques, and new technology to bring down the cost of construction. The construction unions have fought bitterly against these innovations, but unless we make some progressive changes, their members are going to find themselves in the unemployment lines.

"Instead of increasing revenue producers and tax ratables, instead of encouraging new and greater business activity to raise revenue, the city follows the same old path—raising taxes. Someday they're going to have to realize that raising taxes discourages business from coming here and encourages the business that is here to leave. Our tax structure has to be changed. The city income tax and the non-resident tax are only two of the taxes which lead to the exodus of large corporations that employ large numbers of workers.

"New York builders are ready and raring to go," he asserts.

"But they will only use their brains and their money and their muscle if the political atmosphere of the city changes. I have enormous confidence in the business community of New York City. I know what we can do and what we have done. Did you ever realize that the skyline of Manhattan was built not by kings, popes, dictators, or slaves—but by free enterprise?"

Like many other successful entrepreneurs, Sam acquired his skill and knowledge not from textbooks but through experience. His great-grandfather was in the construction business in Paris as far back as 1845, and Sam's father, Harry, continued the tradition after he emigrated to America in 1905. Harry, an architect, had Sam reading blueprints when he was eight years old. "I can remember him spreading a set of plans out on the dining-room table every night after dinner," Sam recalls. "My father gave my two older sisters and me our informal education in the evenings after we had received our formal education during the day. That was my on-the-job training as a youngster."

Sam's son, Richard, who at age thirty-two is the current president of the Lefrak Organization, began learning the business himself at the young age of fourteen. Although a graduate of Columbia Law School, he never intended to practice law. "Richard decided to study law rather than engineering or architecture because so much revolves around the legal issues in our business," Sam explains. "Richard is a highly qualified young man. Although he's not a registered architect or a professional engineer, he has had enough practical experience to have a good working knowledge of those areas."

A broad smile lights up Sam's face. "I pride myself on basically being a teacher," he reflects. "I've trained a lot of guys and put them in the streets. There are always new executives getting on-the-job training in our organization. I tell them they're matriculating at the Lefrak Brick and Mortar College. I teach them how to make decisions, how to evaluate markets, how to get out in the street and see the people.

"I think it's very important for our people to know the 'si-

lent majority.' We've got to get their thinking. I tell my employees, 'You've got to feel what's out there. Then you can
cope with it. *You've got to understand the people.'* I believe
that average guy out there is sophisticated, but insecure, and
we're the ones who are going to give him the security of a
good, affordable place to live."

Not only does Sam understand people, he *loves people.* He
believes that this concern for others is fundamental to his
drive to achieve. "Once an individual learns how to successfully orchestrate his or her own life," he philosophizes, "then he
or she should focus on helping others. I am immensely gratified when I am able to succeed in business and at the same
time contribute to the betterment of other people's lives. I'm
not talking about the medals or the accolades, but about the
personal satisfaction—that's the real reward. If there's a monetary gain, so much the better."

A review of Sam's civic and philanthropic activities shows
the sincerity of his desire to help his fellow man. Only a few of
his extracurricular activities are listed at the beginning of this
chapter. He has served on nearly a hundred different boards
within the local, state, national, and international communities. His charitable contributions run into the millions. He has
demonstrated his willingness to give many causes both his tremendous energy and his financial resources. His community
and business leadership have benefited countless citizens
throughout the world.

A good example of how Sam's commitment to the community and to his businesses can work hand in hand was his company's involvement in 1976 with the Federal Housing Bill in
New York City. Under Section Eight of the bill, funds had
been allocated to relocate elderly citizens out of high crime
areas. The city of New York was diverting this federal money
into its own general fund, but Sam thought the money rightfully belonged to the people. "It was an Act of Congress,
signed by the President, to help the elderly change residences
to safe, secure areas," he explains. "So we went to the bureau-

crats and challenged them in federal court. Housing and Urban Development chief Carla Hills then rejected the city's proposal, and these funds became available for the original purpose of the bill."

The government program, essentially, allows the elderly and poor who qualify for the federal subsidy to seek housing on their own, and not be directed to apartments by any governmental body. The subsidy is available to those who spend at least 40 percent of their monthly income for rent, or who reside in housing that creates a physical or medical hardship.

"We then discovered that many older people would rather live in dangerous and substandard conditions in high crime areas than undergo the emotional hardship of relocation," Sam continues. "They also feared that applying for a Section Eight apartment would involve them with the bureaucracy. We learned, too, that senior citizens not only lacked mobility but lacked access to the normal channels through which they could get information about the program."

To educate the elderly on their rights, the Lefrak Organization placed ads in local and ethnic newspapers and also prepared a film and a talk to be delivered throughout the city at senior citizen centers. Since many senior citizens were afraid to travel on public transport, Sam provided vehicles and security guards to pick up people and bring them to the Lefrak offices.

"We'd get them in our Rescuemobile," Sam says, "and show them the apartments we would have available if they were approved. If they weren't interested in living with us, we'd find housing for them elsewhere. These people were living in high crime areas where their very lives were being threatened. Many of them were shut-ins. We felt this was the right thing to do for people who were unable to help themselves. We not only did it for the aged but also for the mentally retarded. We even went to court when the zoning board told us we couldn't take some of these people who were retarded. Now, they weren't violent, they were just unfortunate.

Some may have had cerebral palsy, others just a lower IQ. But they were all human beings. We created facilities for them where families could take them out of institutions and give them a home environment with some love and affection."

With a look of concern he adds, "We've always believed in helping physically and mentally disabled people. We've also housed a lot of newly arrived immigrants who couldn't find a place to live. I like to address myself to the mass, not to class. People with money can take care of themselves. But we were able to help those who couldn't help themselves get out of the high crime areas and into good, safe communities, where *they* wanted to go. We called the program 'Operation New Life,' and we did it as a public service. We did it by ourselves."

Sam's love of people is matched by his long-standing passion for New York City. Although he is outspoken in his contempt for the city's bureaucrats, Sam remains one of the Big Apple's most loyal supporters. He says discussing the city's future reminds him of a story about the late Supreme Court Justice Oliver Wendell Holmes. "Justice Holmes once got on a train and couldn't locate his ticket." Sam grins. "While the conductor watched, smiling, Justice Holmes searched through all his pockets without success. Finally the conductor, who recognized this distinguished man, said, 'Mr. Holmes, don't worry. You don't need a ticket. You'll probably find it when you get off the train. I'm sure the Pennsylvania Railroad will trust you to mail it to them then.' The Justice looked up at the conductor with some irritation and said, 'My dear man, this is not the problem at all. The problem is not Where is my ticket? The problem is Where am I going?'

"Well, we may not know exactly where New York City is going," Sam booms, "but its greatest days are still ahead. I'll tell you, it's an unbelievable city. I'm a native New Yorker, and despite all the years I've lived here, I still don't know the city. It's more like a country than a city. It has the dynamics, fascination, and intrigue of a small country. It welcomes immigrants, and it gives everybody who wants to work here an opportunity. Visitors from all over the world want to come to the Big Apple."

Sounding like a Chamber of Commerce president, Sam continues: "New York is the nation's leading business center for wholesale, retail, and manufacturing activity. Do you know that there are more major corporations headquartered in this city than in Chicago, Los Angeles, Philadelphia, and Detroit combined? Do you know that the city is the capital of international commerce and finance? That of all foreign corporations with offices in the United States, more than 60 percent have their headquarters in New York City? We have the most comprehensive transportation and distribution system in the country, and one of the world's largest natural harbors. New York is the nation's center for communications, publishing, advertising, legal and financial services, business consulting, and public relations. Both the variety and the reputation of our educational, scientific, and medical complexes are unparalleled. Virtually every skill—industrial, technical, commercial, and professional—is available in the city's huge labor pool. It is, of course, prominent in the visual and performing arts, as well as the fashion industry. With all this and its matchless concentration of cultural and recreational facilities, no wonder New York City is the nation's leading tourist center!"

Sam pauses for a moment to catch his breath. "Naturally young people are attracted to New York. It's all here! There's not another city like it in the world. People just love the excitement of this city. No wonder more and more people are coming back here after they have raised their families. New York is like a magnet. It just keeps right on attracting people. It's a cornucopia holding anything you might want. You can never get bored in this town. There's just no other place like it in the world!"

Despite Sam's enthusiasm for the city, he sees problems in its real estate market. "Today it's very difficult to put up new apartment buildings profitably, because housing is under rent control. That is, it's under the bureaucrats' control. I can't tell you how unfair and inequitable it is. Like anything else politicians regulate, it's counterproductive. But all real estate goes in cycles. Apartment housing is no different. It reminds me of the guy on Seventh Avenue who buys cut velvet because 'everybody's into cut velvet.' Well, my business has its fashions too. Today, office buildings and hotels are very much in the mode.

"But whatever you build, you must focus on your audience," Sam reiterates. "It's not a matter of what you like, but of what *they* need, what *they* like. You can't just arbitrarily decide to put a hotel on a particular piece of property. There might not be a *need* for a hotel at that location. And without location, you have nothing. As I always say, 'In real estate there are three important criteria. The first is location. The second is location. And the third is location.' I don't care if you build the Taj Mahal, if it's on the wrong side of town it's going to be a disappointment. I have often asked people, 'What do you see as the difference between the east side and the west side of New York?' Then I answer my own question with 'The same building on the east side is worth twice what it would be on the west side!' "

Although Sam is involved in real estate transactions across the United States, he is usually identified with the tens of thousands of apartments he constructed in New York in the 1950s and '60s. "In the mid-fifties," he explains, "we set up mass production and were building 20,000 units in a single year! Even Levittown, with all of the publicity it received, only did 11,000 units, and that was over a period of years. We did it from the ground up. We even had control of the source material. We manufactured our own brick, and cut timber from our own forests. I can show you miles of high-rise apartment buildings we developed, as far as the eye can see.

"But, as I mentioned earlier, real estate runs in cycles, and today we don't feel comfortable developing apartment buildings. Of course, things are constantly changing in this business, but right now we're into other activities. For example, we have a hotel on the drawing boards, and we're talking with one of the major hotel operators. At eighty stories, it will be the tallest hotel in the United States. I can't disclose the location, but it's one of the most exciting streets in the city. You'll be able to see both the East and the Hudson rivers and Central Park from its top floors.

"I believe hotels represent the best use of land in New York today," Sam continues. "Tourism is one of our biggest industries, and there's a tremendous shortage of hotel rooms. One reason for the shortage is that many hotels have been converted into apartments and office buildings because that way they qualify for a tax abatement. But hotels are attractive because there are presently no restrictions on rate increases. A customer takes a room for only a day or two, or perhaps a week, but with housing we have rent control and leases that could be a year, two years, or three years. In office buildings, leases are even longer. With a hotel, however, we can raise our rates in the middle of the night for tomorrow's customers."

For twelve years, Sam has been working on one of his greatest undertakings—Battery Park City. When completed it will be the nation's largest urban development. It will be located on a 100-acre Hudson River landfill at the foot of the twin-towered World Trade Center in downtown Manhattan. "The development will have 16,000 apartment units and six million square feet of office space," Sam notes. "Battery Park City will also have two million square feet of shopping and a whole infrastructure of schools, hospitals, and a hotel. It will be a city within the city, 30 million square feet of prime properties.

"We're also doing a very interesting job in SoHo in the West Village. We're taking an old factory and converting it into loft apartments. Each apartment will have a mezzanine and a sleeping loft. We're also in the process of turning a lot of our buildings into co-ops and condominiums. And recently we acquired a half-million-square-foot office building in New

York which somebody else had failed with. We're making it what we think is a huge success. So we're involved in quite a variety of things."

It's mind-boggling to hear Sam tell about all his diverse real estate activities. How can any individual stay on top of so many multimillion-dollar transactions? Sam is quick to credit the dynamic team of top people who have joined his organization over the years. He acknowledges that their expertise is vital; there is no room for an amateur in what he calls the "highly sensitive business" of real estate development. "It's a science," he declares, "not an art."

Without question, it takes a sophisticated businessperson to be successful in all these undertakings. "You have to know everything from A to Z," Sam says matter-of-factly. "You must be a good marketer, merchandiser, designer. You must know quality control. You have to understand the purchasing power of the dollar. You have to be familiar with your markets. And you need to know what the people want.

"In my activities, I've got to be aware of what's coming out of Washington, Albany, and City Hall. There was a time when that wasn't so important. Like the song goes, 'Those were the days, my friend, we thought they'd never end.' But they did end. And it's imperative to stay on top of the constant changes affecting this business. I've got to be aware of everything that may ultimately influence us. That certainly includes politics and economics."

Sam's activities are not confined to the United States. He does business on a worldwide basis. A number of his investments in American real estate have been made jointly with foreign investors. "The United States is the most stable government in the world," Sam points out, "so investors from around the world want to buy good solid American real estate. We invest our own money in every limited and general partnership deal we make with foreigners. Usually we put in 10 percent on the same terms that they do, and I think this gives them comfort." Sam explains that he didn't develop his reputation with the international investment community overnight. "You've got to have the credentials," he stresses. "The Germans, the French, the Japanese—they only trust people with credentials.

"It's good for our economy to bring some of those Deutschmarks, yen, francs, and pounds to America," he adds. "It helps offset our deficit balance of payments. And when foreign money develops American real estate, it creates more work for Americans. That property and whatever is on it is right here; it's a piece of America!"

With his many international banking contacts, Sam is one of the few American developers who finance their real estate holdings in the world money market. "The world is getting smaller and smaller," he notes. "I can pick up the telephone and reach any corner of the globe in a matter of minutes. And although a piece of real estate is always anchored in its particular location, it no longer makes sense to deal only with the local bank. Lefrak International Funding attracts foreign investors and takes advantage of the world money market. With the prime rate at 3 percent in Germany and 2¾ percent in Tokyo, it doesn't make sense to borrow here and pay several times more.

A recent magazine article placed the assets of the privately owned Lefrak Organization at between $600 and $700 million. Refusing to state actual figures, Sam says, "I'm only worth what my banker is ready to loan me." He claims he has no interest in going public, since he believes that a publicly held real estate concern will eventually have trouble satisfying its stockholders. "I run my company for myself and my employees," he declares. "We don't have to cater to the whims of stockholders who demand continual earnings growth."

And, while high leverage is commonplace in the real estate industry, Sam claims to have 75 percent equity with only 25 percent debt service. "I've never had a second mortgage or a ground lease," he asserts. "I own the land under every building I build. We've always operated on our own capital. If we can't afford it, we don't do it! We have a tremendous respect for money. In my estimation, the whole thing is to be able to buy and develop on a non-borrowing basis.

"If you're too highly leveraged," Sam explains, "you're not going to be in this business very long when a recession hits. There's another advantage of having your own money in a project. You pay closer attention to it because you have more to lose. I refer to it as 'Operation Headstart.' This means not putting yourself in a position where you're penalized by too much debt. That's starting out with a severe handicap.

"When money is cheap, that's the time to borrow. But when it's above, you don't borrow. That's the time to get out; it's the perfect time to sell, and fast, while there are plenty of buyers. This is the time to liquidate and get rid of your debts, so you'll be in a position to acquire assets which will appear on the market at reasonable prices.

"The whole idea is to *buy low and sell high,*" Sam stresses. "And one must always address himself to these questions: When should I sell? When should I buy? When should I be in a holding pattern? Well, this is all intuition. That's the difference between an amateur and a professional in this business—intuition."

Sam recalls that before the 1973–74 recession he traveled extensively in the Scandinavian countries and Russia, and then attended the Common Market Conference and NATO Conference in Brussels. "I predicted a recession in America," he says, "because I witnessed what was happening in Europe. People were living on loose credit—fly now, pay later. They were charging more than they could pay for. I began to suspect that the amount of money available couldn't accommodate the debt. I also saw credit being given to people who didn't have the ability to pay back. And I saw people in this country thinking, If I don't buy now, it will cost more next year. There had to be a break in the equity market. Then interest rates started to go up and adversely affect the bottom line. Cash flow eroded. Energy was threatened by the Middle East. I just sensed a recession coming up.

"So back in late 1972, about six months before the mid-1973 inflation-recession crunch, I called in my treasurer and told him to sell at market value anything we couldn't make a profit on by the end of the year. Then we buttoned up financing for all pending projects, turned down new commitments, sold off excess land, and put the money into certificates of deposit and other liquid assets. And when it happened, I was a buyer and everybody else was a seller. We were able to pick up some tremendous bargains."

In talking to Sam, one senses his self-assurance about all aspects of his business. He is fully knowledgeable in every facet of the real estate industry, and familiar with the broader economic and political patterns that affect his business. Although his enormous real estate portfolio is composed mainly of properties in New York City, perhaps the most competitive of all markets, he's definitely an international entrepreneur. He's done just about everything in real estate and, at age sixty-one, shows no signs of slowing up.

"It seems to me," he affirms, "that it's better to wear out than to rust out! People who choose early retirement and the rocking chair are, to my way of thinking, dropouts."

And although Sam has already accomplished more than the average man would dare to dream about, he shows no signs of resting of his laurels. Perhaps his attitude is best summed up when he says, *"My great work is ahead of me."*

10

Harry B. Helmsley

(HELMSLEY-SPEAR, INC.)

Harry B. Helmsley is the president and owner of Helmsley-Spear, Inc., the largest real estate management and brokerage company in the United States. He owns or has an interest in approximately 500 properties throughout the country with a market value in excess of $3 billion.

When Harry joined the firm as an errand boy in 1925 at age sixteen, the company was called Dwight, Voorhis & Perry, Inc. In 1938, when Harry became a partner, the firm was renamed Dwight, Voorhis & Helmsley, Inc. This was changed to Dwight-Helmsley, Inc., in 1946. In 1955, Spear & Company merged with the firm, and it became known as Helmsley-Spear, Inc.

Headquartered in New York City, Helmsley-Spear, Inc., has offices in Chicago, Detroit, Los Angeles, San Francisco, Orlando, Palm Beach, Houston, Newark, New Jersey, and St. Louis.

Although Harry's best-known property is the landmark Empire State Building in New York City, he has personal investments in more than 35 million square feet of office space throughout the United States. His industrial properties include an additional 20 million square feet.

His holdings represent the cream of New York real estate. Some of them are One Penn Plaza, a 2.5-million-square-foot fifty-seven-story office building; the Graybar Building at 420 Lexington Avenue, containing 1.1 million square feet; 10 Hanover Square, a twenty-one-story office building containing 465,000 square feet; the 968,000-square-foot Lincoln Building at 60 East 42nd Street; 22 Cortlandt Street, a thirty-five-story office building of 600,000 square feet; the 530,000-square-foot Pfizer Building at 235 East 42nd Street; the Garment Center Capital Buildings at 498, 500, and 512 Seventh Avenue with a total of 2 million square feet; the Helmsley Building at 230 Park Avenue with 1.1 million square feet; 140 Broadway with 1.2 million square feet; and 601 West 26th Street with 2 million square feet.

His out-of-state commercial properties include One North Dearborn Street in Chicago; the Roosevelt Building in Los Angeles; the Menlo Park Shopping Center in New Jersey; the Syndicate Trust Building in St. Louis; and many others.

Among his hotel field projects are the "Helmsley Hotels" in New York: the Park Lane Hotel, the St. Moritz Hotel, the Windsor Hotel, the Middletowne Hotel, and the Carlton House. He was also the broker in the sale of the Taft, the Plaza, the Shelton, the Lexington, the Townhouse, and the Wyndham. He is presently constructing the Harley and the Helmsley Palace. When these are completed, he will have 4,400 rooms in New York City alone. His out-of-town hotels, comprising 5,000 rooms, are being incorporated into the Harley chain.

Apartment developments include Windsor Park Apartments and Fresh Meadows in New York City; Parkmerced Apartments in San Francisco; the Wilshire Comstock East and Wilshire Comstock West in Los Angeles; the Horizon House in New Jersey; Arlington Towers in Virginia; the Three Fountains apartment complex in Houston; the Drexelbrook Apartments in Drexel Hill, Pennsylvania; the Palm Beach Towers in Palm Beach, Florida; and many others, with a grand total of 50,000 units. The Parkchester development in New York is one of the largest building complexes in the world, housing over 38,000 people in 171 buildings.

Helmsley's industrial properties include Bush Terminal Buildings and Gair Properties in Brooklyn; the Starrett-Lehigh Building and many loft buildings in Manhattan; the Barclay Building in the Bronx; and the 2.5-million-square-foot Russell Industrial Center in Detroit.

Over the years, Harry has been very active in local, national, and international real estate associations. He is, or has been, on the board of governors of the Real Estate Board of New York; chairman of the board and a director of the Realty Foundation of New York; a member of the American Institute of Real Estate Appraisers; a member of the Institute of Real Estate Management; and a member of the International Real Estate Federation.

His numerous civic activities include being a director of the Economic Development Council of New York City, Inc.; a director of the New York Chamber of Commerce and Industry; a director of the Avenue of the Americas Association; a director of the New York Convention & Visitors Bureau; chairman of the Fifth Avenue Association; a vice president of the Twenty-Third Street Association; a member of the advisory board of the Thirty-Fourth Street–Midtown Association; a vice president of the National Realty Committee, Inc.; and a trustee of the Citizens Budget Commission.

He is a director of the Federation of Protestant Welfare Agencies; a trustee of the New York University Medical Center; and a director of Lincoln Center for the Performing Arts. He serves as a director for the National Council to Combat Blindness, and he is co-chairman of the Annual Fight for Sight Campaign. He is a member of the New York Monthly Meeting of the Religious Society of Friends.

In 1958 he was named the Realty Man of the Year. In 1966, he received the Good Scout Award for Outstanding Community Services from the Boy Scouts of America. In 1973 he received an honorary doctor of laws degree from Pace University's Law School and an honorary doctor of humane letters degree from Brandeis. He received the $24 Award from the Museum of the City of New York in 1979, an award given to the person who did the most for the city during the past year. He is a fellow of Brandeis University and New York University.

In addition to Helmsley-Spear, Inc., he owns the real estate brokerage and management firms of Brown, Harris, Stevens, Inc., and Charles F. Noyes Company, Inc.

Harry was born on March 4, 1909, in New York City. He is a graduate of Evander Childs High School in the Bronx. His wife, Leona, is a senior vice president of Brown, Harris, Stevens, Inc. They live in New York City.

HARRY B. HELMSLEY

New York magazine once described a real estate transaction between Harry Helmsley and the Metropolitan Life Insurance Company as "one institution dealing with another." For years Harry has been revered as the king of real estate. In one of the most competitive fields in the business world, he is considered a legendary figure.

The status he has achieved is even more remarkable considering that he started his career at age sixteen as an errand boy. "When I got out of high school," the slim six-foot-three executive recalls, "I decided that since my grandfather had been successful with some properties he had owned, I would go into the real estate business. I wrote to all of the prominent firms in New York, and ended up as an errand boy with Dwight, Voorhis and Perry in 1925. I've been with the firm ever since."

Founded under the title Samuel B. Goodale in 1866, the prominent real estate management and brokerage company had changed names several times throughout the years. After various changes in personnel, the firm became Helmsley-Spear, Inc., in 1955, with Harry Helmsley at the helm.

Harry recalls that he was soon "promoted" to office boy

and later to rent collector. "There's no question about it," he proclaims, "I got fantastic on-the-job training as I moved from one phase of the business to another. After being a rent collector, I became manager of a couple of buildings, and from that I went into the renting field. In those days, our firm was strictly a managing agent. Because of the depression, buying and selling of real estate had come to a standstill. So, during the 'thirties, I managed and rented properties for the big institutions like Metropolitan Life and New York Life.

"In 1938, when there appeared to be some movement in the market, I began selling real estate and forming syndicates for some of my friends. By this time, the institutions which had held on to their properties for so long had lost all confidence in real estate. They were so anxious to get rid of their properties that they were selling with 10 percent cash down and 3 percent interest on the mortgage. So if you knew the market, you could find some good buys. Then it became a matter of knowing how to manage those properties better than the institutions had."

Harry was in his late twenties when he acquired his first properties. His early investments were modest ones, generally made by using his commissions for a down payment. "A good illustration," he recalls, "was a building I picked up back in 1938. The price was $1,000 for the deed on top of a $100,000 mortgage. This meant that for $1,000 in cash I could get control of a $101,000 property. Eventually I sold the property for $165,000—a good return on a $1,000 investment.

"Another example was a $65,000 property which I bought with a partner for 10 percent down—only $6,500 in cash. Well, my commission was 5 percent, so I just threw my commission into the deal. We eventually sold that property for $180,000.

"In those days you didn't need as much cash as you do today. *I got in with effort.* It took a tremendous amount of effort, but it could be done. One reason it was possible to make these deals was that the institutions were really anxious to dispose of their properties. As a matter of fact, the banks and savings and loans were required by a state mandate to sell their foreclosures within a ten-year period. They had to get rid of properties they had foreclosed in 1930."

Harry did not rely only on the knowledge he gained through experience; he studied real estate. "I took practically every course you could take on the subject," he says, "starting with the principles of real estate. I became a Certified Property Manager (CPM), and I became a member of the American Institute of Real Estate Appraisers. I suppose I have every degree you can get in real estate. Appraising is one of the most useful areas I ever studied. It gave me the skills to analyze properties' values when I was considering making a purchase or forming a syndicate."

A highly motivated, aggressive young man, Harry became a partner in 1938. "It didn't take much capital to become a partner," Harry says, "because the business wasn't really worth that much. The company didn't own any properties, and during the depression years there hadn't been enough sales to generate commissions of any consequence. The firm was just eking out an existence.

"As a matter of fact, Helmsley-Spear, Inc., doesn't own any properties today," he explains. "We never did own; we manage. As an individual, I do own real estate through Helmsley Enterprises. I own some properties outright and have a partial interest in others. In some cases I'm in a partnership arrangement, and you just name it, we've done it. Helmsley Enterprises has structured practically every kind of deal imaginable."

The friendly low-keyed conservatively dressed man is said to have put together more real estate deals than anyone else in the industry. He explains that post–World War II inflation greatly increased the value of his holdings. During the same period, Americans developed a desire to own real estate. Harry states simply, "This is really how I got started." Once he had accumulated some wealth to accompany his vast knowledge, Harry Helmsley was on his way to becoming one of the great self-made men of modern times.

Harry always studies a property in minute detail prior to negotiating a transaction. When purchasing an existing office building, he emphasizes, "you must be so familiar with the market that you know automatically whether the rents are too high or too low. It's dangerous to invest when you don't have that kind of knowledge. An individual who just decides to get into real estate and who has no background has no way of knowing whether the rents are low or the price of the property is just too high. You must analyze the entire rental income and look at the expiration dates of your leases to determine what the rents should be.

"Because we have so many properties, we can put a potential purchase on a scale to determine what it should cost to operate. This makes it easy for us to analyze. But after we've analyzed it," he stresses, "we always consider that information *past history*. It doesn't mean a great deal to us, because in real estate we're not dealing with the past. We're dealing with what's going to happen *tomorrow*. So we try to get a good feel for what the rents will be when those leases expire. And, fortunately for us, we generally come out pretty well in this respect."

When asked what he considers the most important factor in a real estate transaction, Harry quickly replies, "Location, location, location. I know it's trite, but it's true. I don't think I would ever take a property that wasn't well located and that, in my opinion, didn't have a bright future. Just analyze our properties, and you'll discover that we have the best buildings in the best locations!"

Although the Helmsley organizations have the most up-to-date computers, Harry insists that the computers are mainly used for bookkeeping and preparing statements. "The computer has no judgment," he states. "It can give you the numbers, but those numbers won't tell you what's going to happen. In the final analysis, it's judgment that counts."

Harry's wife, Leona, his biggest supporter, says about her husband, "Harry is a mathematical genius. He's absolutely incredible. His mind is like a computer. He could tell you every fact about every real estate transaction he's ever been involved in. But his real talent is his judgment. He almost always comes up with simple answers to seemingly complex problems. I refer to him as 'the judge,' because when I have a problem that seems insurmountable and I go to Harry, he comes up with a simple solution in a matter of minutes. He does the same thing in real estate, and the simple solutions are usually the best ones."

Among his peers, Harry has the long-standing reputation of being a very decisive individual whose decisions are always right. "I think what I do best"—he ponders—"is make up my mind to buy a piece of property—because I have complete confidence in my own infallibility." He breaks into a friendly laugh. "And when I'm ready to go ahead and make a deal, I don't have to convince anybody. I don't have to be a salesman. If I have a good deal, everybody wants to get aboard. I take a lead position in every deal. I can take a major stake of $5 million, $10 million, $30 million—whatever is necessary in order to consummate the deal. When others see how much I believe in it, they want to participate too."

Over the years, Harry has established one of the finest reputations in American business. The world of real estate recognizes his handshake as the guarantee of a firm deal. He is reputed to have never reneged on any deal which simply involved a handshake, and this includes many transactions worth millions of dollars.

Harry offers this advice on acquiring a property: "You must decide what it's worth to you, and how high you're willing to go. Then, when that figure is reached, you must stop! There's no point in just bidding for the sake of owning the property. Of course, various strategies must be considered in structuring the financing, because that can either make or break a deal. The length of your mortgage is important and, naturally, how much cash you need to come up with. Many times a deal will depend on where you can get new, fresh mortgage money. Sometimes it's necessary to buy the property for all cash, and structure the financing later. There's a tremendous number of different ways to do it, and I would venture to say that most of your strategy is dependent on how you work out the financing."

He states with strong conviction that he never personally signs on a mortgage. "That's a good way to go broke. The lending institution has the property as collateral for the mortgage, and I think that's all they're entitled to. Actually, in the state of New York, it's presumed that the value of the property is there, and it's almost against public policy to go against the note. Unless, of course, the bank can prove they loaned more than the value of the property because of the signature. But, regardless of presumption, I won't sign."

While many would-be investors shy away from large real estate ventures, Harry maintains that there's really not a great deal of difference between the "big ones" and the "little ones." He grins when asked to compare a large transaction to a small one. "It's the same deal, except you just add another naught here and there.

"Actually," he continues in a more serious tone, "it's really easier to make a $6.5 million deal than a $65,000 deal. It's just a question of how many naughts you have. The business principles are the same. It's also easier to run a larger building. We can generate more income, and consequently hire better people."

"Thinking big" has become a Helmsley trademark. Perhaps the crown jewel in the string of multimillion-dollar Helmsley properties is the Empire State Building. Harry acquired it in 1961 when he and a longtime friend and business associate, Lawrence A. Wien, headed a group of investors. It was a seven-year-long brokerage transaction. The $85 million involved included $33 million in cash, raised from 3,300 investors who each put down $10,000. "We just divided it up the same way

Wall Street does," Harry says matter-of-factly. "They put out an issue and millions of people take a fractional interest."

Harry claims he wouldn't take $200 million for the Empire State Building today. "I really don't know what it's worth," he states. "Since it's not for sale, I'm not getting any offers."

Helmsley's "thinking big" extends to residential investment too. The realty community was awed in 1968 when Harry led a group to purchase Parkchester, at that time the largest building complex in the world. Parkchester, located in the Bronx, had originally been built for an investment by the Metropolitan Life Insurance Company. The complex represented a $90 million deal. Its 171 apartment buildings contain 12,271 units, housing 38,000 people. Among its other conveniences, Parkchester has more than 100 stores.

One Penn Plaza represents another of Harry's multifaceted real estate ventures. It soars 57 stories above Manhattan's West Side, just across from Madison Square Garden. As the developer and managing partner of Mid-City Associates (One Penn Plaza's owners), Harry negotiated a fifty-year $200 million ground lease on the site, with three twenty-five year renewal options. The towering office building opened in 1973, a time when the real estate boom of the 1960s was definitely coming to an end. The national economy, troubled by inflation and by the imposition and later the removal of wage and price controls, was on its way to the deepest recession since World War II. The energy crisis, only a few months away, would accelerate the recession and at the same time send building operating costs to all-time highs. These conditions would put New York's office-leasing market into its worst slump in decades. Manhattan was being billed as the burial ground for a new breed of white elephants—high-rise office buildings.

As One Penn Plaza opened its doors to tenants, its major tenant, Ebasco, which had been taken over by Boise Cascade Corporation, had cancelled its lease of 700,000 square feet. The 2.5-million-square-foot structure opened with a minuscule 11 percent occupancy! At a time when millions of square feet of office space had become available in the New York market, filling up One Penn Plaza loomed as a Herculean task.

The Helmsley-Spear leasing department incorporated creative marketing ideas and introduced innovative programs. A major promotional effort, which included advertising, brochures, direct mail, and publicity, was directed at real estate brokers and potential tenants. The message was based on "supplying tenants with the kind of product they need to reach their business goals." When large tenants couldn't be attracted, the step (unheard-of for a new building) was taken of tailoring leasing plans and space to the needs of smaller tenants. The program was successful; by the end of the first year, the building's occupancy was at 50 percent.

The marketing programs emphasized One Penn Plaza's unique location. It stands at the center of a vast public transportation network. Direct indoor access is available to commuter trains to Long Island and New Jersey; long-distance trains to New England, the South, and the West; four subway lines; and the PATH system to New Jersey. The locale is also served by eleven bus lines. There are convenient auto routes to the tunnels and airports, and the Port Authority Bus Terminal is within walking distance. The building's location at the city's transportation center was one of its strongest selling points. The convenience it offered enabled tenants to attract personnel from throughout the greater New York metropolitan area.

Another point the leasing team emphasized was the skyscraper's extensive modern facilities. Equipment was installed to support the engineering needs of tenants with complex computer and communications installations. This capability attracted several early tenants who leased large amounts of space. For example, Delta Air Lines took 80,000 square feet for its regional reservation center, which uses highly technical communications equipment. The building houses a number of restaurants, including the famous Toots Shor's. It has forty-six high-speed elevators, and there is air-conditioning throughout its attractive halls and lobbies. An interior loading dock accommodates ten trucks simultaneously. A permanently installed window-washing scaffold and rig operates year round. Valet parking is available at the building's 700-car garage.

One Penn Plaza also has Helmsley-Spear offices on the premises. The on-site management staff is available to help tenants with their problems and to give them a way to directly contact the building's owners. It includes experienced leasing brokers, engineers, maintenance personnel, and other specialists. Such an on-site staff, a practice of the company, ensures efficient property management and provides tenants with the best possible service.

One Penn Plaza now has an occupancy rate of 100 percent. The potential disaster was turned into one of Manhattan's most successful office buildings. Its story illustrates the talents of Harry Helmsley and his management team. They were put to the test and came through with flying colors. Another thing this success story demonstrates is the patience and perseverance an office-building developer must have in order to complete a project successfully. Of course, as Harry is quick to point out, the job is never finished. Full occupancy is maintained only by continual servicing.

Harry also notes, "We have about seventy-five people in our rental office constantly out there knocking on doors. They keep files on the expiration dates of prospective tenants' leases, and they follow up on them like clockwork. These people are continually making personal contacts and giving presentations to offer space in our buildings."

The distinguished-looking executive leans back in his chair and says in a tone somewhat louder than his normally soft voice, "I think office space is great property to own in New York. It may be slightly more difficult to operate, but those long-term leases are nice, especially compared to residential leases. You know, I wouldn't take a lease for less than fifteen years in a new building. Long-term leases like that make it possible for us to get a proper mortgage, and in many cases permit us to completely borrow out.

"Now I'm involved with many out-of-town office buildings, but the market is different outside New York City," Harry continues. "Companies are more conservative elsewhere, and it's difficult to sign them up for more than a five-year lease. Because the tenant can always find another spot when that lease expires, you can't use such a short-term lease as a basis for financing. You always have to worry that in five years, when their lease is up, somebody is going to woo them away with a better deal. Then you'd have the expense of remodeling and making alterations to suit the new tenant. So, as I said, while office buildings are very good in Manhattan, they can be a headache in other markets."

In developing a high-rise office building, it is important to attract major tenants prior to actual construction. As Harry puts it, "I like to see 40 percent of the building leased up before I break ground. I don't like to start without having a bell-wether. I figure that if I can get 40 percent leased, I can get the other 60 percent. Of course, today's high interest rates and high construction costs make it even more desirable to have tenants before you build."

When questioned about the higher rents a new office building must demand because of the high cost of development, Harry explains, "A tenant will only pay these high rents when there's no other space available. Right now in New York there's just no space uptown, and what's available downtown is being rapidly eaten up. Whereas two years ago it was difficult to get $12 a foot because there were a lot of vacancies, today you can get $20 a foot because of the shortage of space. It's strictly a matter of supply and demand. It has absolutely nothing to do with whether the company can afford it or not, although the tenants *can* afford it, because business in the United States is so good. True, no businessman is going to pay a high rent when he could pay less next door. But when there's no next door, he has to pay. You don't fold a business because the rent goes up."

Harry adds without batting an eye, "Space in a new office building is going for $20 a square foot today. And prime office space is as high as $30 per square foot. As for the store space on the ground floor, it's $100 and up, depending on location. Fifth Avenue, for instance, is a good $150 a foot. And even at these rates the available space in the newer buildings is practically nil.

"One thing that a new office building has going for it," he continues, "is that today the major companies need large units on adjoining floors. In an older building, unless somebody has vacated overnight, that kind of space is never available. So if the company is, for instance, an IBM, an AT&T, or a large bank, and they want contiguous space of 300,000 to 400,000 square feet, it has to be built for them."

Harry mentions that while a large corporation occasionally enters a joint venture with an office-building developer, such partnerships are less frequent than most people think. "There's more talk about them than there are actual joint ventures. It's not so easy to put one together. You must remember that such companies really don't want to be in the real estate business. While from my point of view it's a tax shelter, they'd rather lease than own; rent is completely deductible, but depreciation reduces a company's earnings on its profit-and-loss statement."

Another misconception about the real estate market is that there are large numbers of foreign investors buying American properties. "I think there's more talk about that than actual deals being closed," comments Harry, who perhaps has better firsthand knowledge than anyone else. "The foreign investors spend a lot of time looking. After all, we have a stable political system, and this is one of the few places in the world where they can feel safe in putting their money. But they just don't buy. The great majority of all purchases today are made by Americans, primarily by the pension funds and the insurance companies. They've gone into the equity market in a big way in recent years."

Although the thought of American properties being purchased by foreign investors disturbs many Americans, Harry remarks with a shrug, "I guess they're as good at being landlords as anyone else. What can they do? They can collect the rents. And if your complaint is that they're overpaying and boosting the market, then you can buy and sell out to them!"

While nobody likes inflation, Harry says it doesn't hurt his business nearly as much as it does others. "The value of our buildings increases faster than inflation," he says, "because of the increasing cost of construction. And, of course, the value of land rises as less and less is available. When inflation hurts us is when the office-building rental market is bad. Our operating costs continue. Our wages go up; our electricity goes up; the cost of fuel is incredible! So eventually we're forced to raise rents. It's like a seesaw. One minute we're ahead of expenses and the next minute there's an oversupply of space and we can't get the rent we should be getting."

Still, Harry says, owners of office buildings have some protection against this seesaw. "Since there's no rent control with office buildings, we can pass increased expenses along," he explains. "Our leases also have a cost-of-living index which protects us against the devaluation of the dollar. Housing is another story. It's become a political football. Rent controls have made it impossible to get a decent return on apartment houses.

"Today I think hotels bring in the best return of any property in New York. There really seems to be a need for hotels in the city right now. I have almost 3,000 hotel rooms in Manhattan. During the week they're just about fully rented, and on some days I don't have a single room available. With all the business people and foreign dignitaries and tourists who visit the Big Apple, there's always a market for a hotel that offers outstanding amenities and protects their privacy."

Harry displayed uncanny vision when he opened the Park

Lane Hotel in 1971, during a period when New York City's overall hotel occupancy rate was reported at 68 percent and dropping. As the sole owner, he invested between $30 and $35 million in the 640-room hotel located at a prestigious Central Park South address. It was New York's first new hotel in seven years, and at the time the "experts" predicted that it would be the last for the rest of the decade.

When asked why he built the Park Lane, Harry replies, "I believe in New York, and I thought the timing was right for a new luxury hotel in a first-class neighborhood. I wanted to emphasize excellent service, elegant decor, and absolute respect for the guest's privacy. At a time when most hotels depend on convention and commercial business to turn a profit, I intentionally limited the size of the ballroom to 200 to spare the guests the noise and confusion this type of business brings."

Harry presently has two major hotels under construction in Manhattan: the Harley, a thirty-eight-story 800 room hotel on 42nd Street just off Third Avenue, and the Palace, a 1,000-room grand hotel with a price tag of about $80 million. Located on Madison Avenue across from St. Patrick's Cathedral, the fifty-one-story Palace will be the city's tallest hotel, and as Harry puts it, "I assume it will be New York's finest."

Although hotels represent the best potential return on investment of all New York properties, Harry says "the difficulty with hotels lies in financing them. With an office building, if we can achieve 100 percent occupancy prior to construction, we can borrow out, so we have tremendous leverage. But with a hotel, the financial institutions don't lend more than 75 percent or so. So hotels require a large capital investment. But it's worth the risk. A successful hotel will generate a fantastic yield on the money put into it."

When asked what he considers his greatest accomplishment, Harry, who is usually quick to respond, hesitates. At last he replies that the Empire State Building is a favorite, "especially because it is a famous landmark," and he adds, "It was also a very interesting, creative deal, particularly in terms of the financing.

"But it's one thing to own a building, and it's another thing to *build* and own it," he continues. "I got a big kick out of building the Park Lane Hotel, but then, of course, I'm getting a big kick out of building the Palace Hotel and the Harley Hotel."

There is a warm, playful side to Harry which doesn't necessarily surface during a tough real estate negotiation. A case in point is the naming of the new Harley Hotel and the 5,000-room Harley chain. The idea for the name goes back several years to Harry's honeymoon in the Mediterranean. His wife, Leona, was thrilled with the 136-foot yacht he chartered for the trip. "Do you like it?" Harry asked. "Like it? I *love* it!" she answered. "Well then, we'll buy it and name it the SS *Lee Har*," he promised. "Since it's your money, darling, let's call it the SS *Har Lee*," she replied.

After a week at sea, Leona was so sick of boats that nothing would get her aboard a yacht again. So, as a substitute for a boat, the Helmsleys installed a ship's steering wheel on the terrace of their Palm Beach penthouse overlooking Lake Worth. Life preservers and other decor have SS HAR LEE inscribed on them. As Leona puts it, "We can just turn the wheel and go anywhere we want, and we never get seasick." Later, when Harry needed a name for his hotel chain, the couple used "Harley." "But, at Leona's suggestion, we changed the spelling and put a letter 'y' on it," Harry says with a laugh.

Leona thinks that their nicest times are spent at Palm Beach, where they can be alone together. "We don't go out socially while we're there," she says, "and we're in the ocean every day. We're probably the only two people in the entire Atlantic Ocean over twelve years old who ride the waves on rafts," she jokes. "But it's fun, and it's great exercise."

The couple regularly swim in the pool they had installed in their penthouse at the Park Lane. "Harry is in top physical condition," Leona notes with pride, "and he's also a wonderful dancer. An evening out dancing is one of our greatest plea-sures. People who see him say that he's the most beautiful dancer they've ever seen."

There is a tendency for people to think that one of the world's leading real estate magnates would have little time to devote to non-business activities. But the party given for Har-ry by his wife and attended by hundreds of friends every year shows another aspect of this fascinating man. This birthday party is considered *the* party of the year in New York. "We have about 200 guests," Leona explains. "The governor comes, and the mayor; *everybody's* there. We have cocktails in our penthouse at seven-thirty, and around nine we go down-stairs to the ballroom for a sitdown dinner. Everybody wears a button that says, 'I'm Just Wild About Harry,' and Harry's says 'I'm Harry.' We have a sixteen-piece orchestra, and they play 'I'm Just Wild About Harry' when he enters the room. Everybody stands up and joins in with the singing. And at in-tervals throughout the evening 5,000 balloons are released. Everything has the 'I'm Just Wild About Harry' theme. One year the back of the menu depicted Harry playing Monopoly with his buildings, such New York landmarks as the Empire State Building, One Penn Plaza, the Park Lane, and the Carl-ton House. Another year the menu showed Harry as Super-man, flying over New York City. This time it read, 'He's a Superman.' "

The song "I'm Just Wild About Harry" has become *his* song, and is often played at banquets and dinner parties when Harry enters the room. When, at a recent opening at Radio City Music Hall, the song was played as part of a musical re-vue, the eyes of the Helmsleys' friends in the audience turned to Harry. "How do you like that?" somebody shouted. "Leo-na even arranged for *them* to play his song!"

Harry's real estate, civic, and philanthropic activities are more involved today than ever. One project presently under way is the construction of luxury condominium apartments on elegant Brickell Avenue in Miami. And just recently Harry purchased from Standard Oil of Ohio the Hospitality Motor

Inns, a chain of fourteen hotels and thirty-five restaurants. When questioned about what's next, Harry responds simply, "Whatever comes along. I don't have any definite game plan. I'll take the deal that looks best, and I don't know which one it's going to be tomorrow."

It's safe to assume that Harry Helmsley will make many deals in the future. A healthy seventy years old, he shows no sign of slowing down. "I'm fortunate in being surrounded by a fine group of people"—he smiles—"so it's really fun to come to work. We're all working together for the same goal. Granted, the goal is making money, but that's really not such a bad thing; we're producing something and making a contribution to society. I like to do what's good for New York, and I think the whole country benefits when we do."

The 1.1-million-square-foot Helmsley Building at 230 Park Avenue is a good example of how Harry frequently combines good business and civic practices. This grand old beaux arts–style building reflects the elaborate design of the 1920s. In 1978, Harry had the entire exterior of the building steam-cleaned and gilded. Magnificent statues, brilliantly lit at night, adorn the building. Its new appearance has made it one of New York's showplaces, even recognizable from airplanes flying over the city. Cab drivers point it out with pride, and Harry has received thousands of letters thanking him for this beautiful improvement to the city. Only after his wife insisted, did he consent to allow the building to bear his name. "Other men have buildings named after them," Leona says, "and after how hard Harry has worked for New York City, I felt that one building should be named for him."

When he's asked, "Why do you work so hard? Why do you want more money?" Harry replies, "I have to admit that the money isn't really going to change the way I live. When you get to a certain point, there's no way you can spend more money. But it's the only way to keep score. Without it, how would you know whether you're succeeding? Of course, money gives me the ability to do things I couldn't do otherwise. To build a Palace Hotel, you have to have the capital. And it's a great feeling to take a whole block and create a beautiful building on it. I get the same feeling from the ownership of other properties. It's tremendously satisfying to know we've got some of the best properties in the country."

From his office on the fifty-third floor of the Lincoln Building, at 60 East 42nd Street, Harry keeps a close watch on his New York real estate. He has a breathtaking view of many of his properties, including the majestic Empire State Building. The view from his two-story penthouse in the Park Lane is also magnificent. "I just look out my window"—he chuckles—"and I keep a close watch on my inventory."

Harry generally arrives at the office at 9:00 A.M. and leaves about 5:00 P.M. "But I never go home without a briefcase," he notes. "I work a few hours each evening or in the morning before I come to the office. I also get a lot accomplished over the weekends."

How does his wife react to her husband spending so much time on his work? "I'm blessed to have a great wife," he says. "She's not only beautiful and dynamic, she understands. Of course, Leona's been in real estate herself for about eighteen years.

"She was a competitor of mine, so I took her on as a senior vice president of Brown, Howard, Stevens, Inc. Then the only way I could see to get out of my contract with her was to marry her. So we got married and I tore up the contract." He laughs. "We're always together. It's a big help to have somebody who understands your business, and to be able to talk to her about it."

Will Harry Helmsley ever retire? Not very likely. "As long as I've got my health, I'll just keep right on going," he asserts. "I'm having so much fun, I don't know what I could do that would give me as much pleasure. If I retired, I'd end up playing a bad game of golf. I'd rather have a good game of real estate."

Conclusion

Perhaps now that you have become acquainted with the people in this book, you no longer think of the real estate business as being strictly land, minerals, trees, fences, bricks, and mortar. Instead, you will see it as a *people business.* And some of the most interesting success stories in America are about the people who have carved out flourishing careers in this field.

As the value of real estate has continued to outpace inflation, the public interest in owning property has risen steadily. Everybody seems to want to own a piece of America. The demand by foreign investors shows how far the fever has spread. So interest in real estate is not limited to the nation's 2.1 million licensed agents. The craze has reached far and wide.

However, each of these ten individuals has emphasized one point: Either develop an expertise in real estate or *stay away!* This is not a business for amateurs. While fortunes have been made, they have also been lost. And while successful real estate people can generate immense incomes, many others within the industry are struggling just to earn a decent living.

When it comes to investing, Harry Helmsley, the dean of real estate dealers, says, "You must be so familiar with the market that you know automatically whether the rents are too high or low. It's dangerous to invest when you don't have that kind of knowledge. An individual who just decides to get into real estate and who has no background has no way of knowing whether the rents are low or the price of the property is just too high." He says that he always studies a property in minute detail prior to negotiating a transaction.

And, as Sam LeFrak explains, there are also other areas the successful investor must be knowledgeable about. "In my activities I've got to be aware of what's coming out of Washington, Albany, and City Hall." He stresses that it is imperative to stay on top of changing legislation that may ultimately influence the business. Every political and economic issue which may affect real estate is carefully scrutinized by Sam and his people. When he says, "That's the difference between an amateur and a professional in this business—intuition," he is fully cognizant of the fact that training, education, and experience are the basic ingredients necessary to acquire "intuition."

Of course, each of the brokers also emphasized the importance of education and training in developing a successful agency. Without question, this was their attraction for new agents and the cornerstone on which they built their large sales organizations. Mary Bell Grempler says, "We were the first firm in our area that had a procedure book. I realized that a tremendous void existed in Baltimore in developing new agents." Ebby Halliday believes that sales associates are attracted to her company because of the supportive training services it offers. Ebby Halliday, Realtors, uses the latest technology, including remote-controlled rear-screen projection for slides and motion pictures, a stereo sound system, and special video equipment. The firm has a full-time training manager with two assistants, and frequent educational seminars to keep all agents well abreast of the changes within the industry.

Gordon Gundaker states, "Right from the beginning, our major emphasis has been placed on properly educating our sales force." He too has an in-house training department and modern equipment to present educational information to his agents. Recently he spent more than $25,000 to purchase videotape programs. "Education is a continuing process," Gordon emphasizes. "You can't ever let down, because this is an ever-changing business. If you stop developing your educational program, you begin to slip backwards." Ralph Pritchard also believes in the importance of education. Thorsen Realtors has a highly sophisticated training program for its new agents, as well as a strong continuing education program for experienced sales associates. In addition, Ralph has been involved in various educational activities in both local and national associations. Arthur Bartlett stresses that one of Century 21's strong selling points is the training and educational material it provides the small broker—material that only the big broker could afford in the past.

All ten of these individuals are service-oriented. Bettye Hardeman says matter-of-factly, "I suppose wanting to serve people is just my nature. I'm proud to serve people. I think people know when you care, and I do truly care." Her long work hours show her devotion to the business. "I'm like a doctor," she says "on call twenty-four hours a day, seven days a week. Serving clients means showing a home whenever it is convenient for them. I work seven days a week, and they're full days, too."

Phyllis Burhenn also works seven days a week and often doesn't get home until nine or ten in the evening. Like Bettye, she is service-minded. "I thrive on being able to help people," she says. "I've put many people into a home who thought they could never afford one. Sometimes creative financing has made the difference for a family between owning and renting a home. I get a tremendous amount of satisfaction out of this business when I can help people."

The brokers are equally concerned with service. "We're constantly telling our salespersons that it's not the money involved, but *helping people* that really counts," Gordon Gundaker emphasizes. He explains that his firm writes to all clients asking whether the service they received from Gundaker Realtors was satisfactory. "Our customer relations manager will follow up and call every customer who doesn't send the letter back," Gordon explains. "It used to be that somebody would be walking around with something in their craw, and we didn't know about it. A few months later, one of our people would bump into him in the hardware store, and he'd say, 'Boy, you really sold me a dog!' Today we avoid situations like that because we're following up on every transaction to make certain that people are satisfied."

Thorsen Realtors will do anything to satisfy an unhappy customer. "If a buyer has problems with the house, we'll solve the problems. If it's the wrong house, we'll offer to sell it for him at no cost," Ralph Pritchard asserts. "It's much better to have a guy out there saying to everyone, 'Boy, did I get treated right at Thorsen,' than to have him grousing about how lousy we are. We don't want customers saying, 'Those people don't know what they're doing.' We don't need that kind of publicity. In some cases we have even offered to buy the house back."

Ebby Halliday stresses communications as the key to servicing clients. "Inform! Inform! Inform!" she declares. "We never forget that real estate is a service business. All real estate firms sell the same product, so service is what separates us from our competition." Mary Bell Grempler makes the same point. "With the multiple listings," she says, "we're going to have the exact same product as anybody else. It's only a matter of who gives the customer the best service. I think that's our whole competitive edge."

Servicing the *entire* community is also a high priority, as witnessed by the enormous commitment of both time and money to non–real estate activities. While heavy work schedules don't permit as much extracurricular involvement during the early stages of a successful career, once they are established, real estate people tend to become very active. In addition to civic and charitable involvements, most devote time and energy to state and national real estate associations. In fact, Ebby Halliday, Ralph Pritchard, Ernest Hahn, Samuel LeFrak, and Harry Helmsley participate in an array of community, civic, and association activities too extensive to list in their biosketches!

Without question, these people share a common philosophy regarding service to the general community. It is expressed well by Ebby Halliday, who believes that the most effective real estate people live in the community where they work. "I think a hometown, home-founded, home-owned real estate company is in the best possible position to serve the community. *A good real estate person has an obligation to put something back into the community.* After all, that community is his or her inventory. In our business, we help attract people to live in an area and rear their families there. Our vested interest in the community means we have a responsibility to give it additional time, energy, and money. The community's well-being is our well-being. The community's health is our health."

Ralph Pritchard calls it "community penetration." He explains, "We encourage our people to be active in their communities, and most of them are key contributors to various kinds of projects at the local level. They may be in service clubs, church activities, education, bowling leagues, whatever. The relationship between real estate agents and the neighborhood is very important. Buyers and sellers feel better about dealing with agents they know."

Evidently, serving the community is a key ingredient in becoming successful in real estate. And the more successful real estate people are, the more time they manage to commit to worthy causes. Certainly the entire community benefits from the participation of these highly capable individuals.

So it can be said that successful real estate people have found it profitable to think in terms of what's good for their customers and for society in general. And the fact that such an approach works is one of the great strengths of the free enterprise system. As Harry Helmsley puts it, "Granted, the goal is making money, but that's really not such a bad thing; we're producing something and making a contribution to society. I like to do what's good for New York, and I think the whole country benefits when we do."

Ernest Hahn also takes great pride in the contribution his shopping centers make to the communities where they are located. "We build what the people want and like instead of what the developer wants and likes," he stresses. "Too often, the developer is merely expressing *his* desires instead of the people's." His policy of thinking in terms of community benefit is evidenced by his statement, "We believe that it's a company's responsibility to soften the blow of a new center which is going to produce a great deal of traffic and masses of people in one place; we don't want to have a harsh impact on the community." He adds, *"It's their center."*

I believe that much of what motivates these ten individuals is their *love of people.* I think Sam LeFrak puts it best when he says, "Once an individual learns how to successfully orchestrate his or her own life, then he or she should focus on helping others. I am immensely gratified when I am able to succeed in business and at the same time contribute to the betterment of other people's lives. I'm not talking about the medals or the accolades, but about the personal satisfaction— that's the real reward. If there's monetary gain, so much the better."

While profit is not a dirty word in real estate, it is obviously not the only important factor in business decisions. The business affairs of these real estate people are clearly influenced by their love of people and their concern for the community. Such altruism seems to grow during the course of a successful career. Ebby Halliday shows this spirit when she talks proudly of putting her 10,000-square-foot office building on a lot zoned for a twenty-story building. "It just makes good economic sense to build a high-rise on it," she says, "but we elected not to, because we believed this area shouldn't have that kind of a building. I suppose I get great satisfaction in making a bum decision once in a while strictly for aesthetic reasons."

In addition to being involved in building a better community, each of these real estate people takes tremendous pride in his or her hometown. Sam LeFrak sums up his feelings about New York when he says enthusiastically, "It's all here! There's not another city like it in the world. . . . New York is like a magnet. It just keeps right on attracting people. It's a cornucopia holding anything you might want. You can never get bored in this town. There's just no other place like it in the world!"

Ebby Halliday supports the "Big D" every bit as wholeheartedly as Sam LeFrak does the "Big Apple." Often described as a second Chamber of Commerce, Ebby Halliday, Realtors, distributes *Welcome to Dallas* kits to out-of-towners interested in relocating to the area. Wherever I went to interview these real estate people—Baltimore, Atlanta, Chicago, St. Louis, California—I found this kind of enthusiasm. If these ten people are representative, then it can be concluded that one important prerequisite to success in real estate is to be *sold* on the territory where you sell.

Their enthusiasm is not confined to their hometowns. These are people who find their work exciting and fulfilling. Phyllis Burhenn says, "I love my work. I *really* love it. I'd rather sell real estate than go to the beach or play cards." Ebby Halliday feels the same way about her work. She says, "I still get just as excited about this business. Even a small transaction is just as much a thrill today as ever." And Ralph Pritchard asserts, "There's a thrill in selling a piece of real estate—bringing a buyer and seller together—which is almost unreal. This is especially true when it's been a tough deal. Every real estate salesman has had this experience—we all get that special thrill out of selling a property." As Emerson put it, "Nothing is more contagious than enthusiasm." These people love their work, and their excitement spreads to those around them.

Yes, they love real estate, and it's doubtful that any of them would ever willingly give it up. When retirement is mentioned, Harry Helmsley says, "As long as I've got my health, I'll just keep right on going. I'm having so much fun, I don't know what I could do that would give me as much pleasure. If I retired, I'd end up playing a bad game of golf. I'd rather have a good game of real estate." And Sam LeFrak declares, "It's better to wear out than to rust out. People who choose early retirement and the rocking chair are, to my way of thinking, dropouts." Although Sam has already accomplished more than the average person would dare dream about, he has not finished yet. He's still working as hard as ever, and he will continue to as long as he can. Not a man to rest on his laurels, he says emphatically, "My great work is ahead of me."

Of course, retirement is the farthest thing from the mind of any reader contemplating or just beginning a career in real estate. If that's you, prepare to devote long hours to your work. It is a field which demands total commitment. And while it may be discouraging at first, don't give up. It usually takes time to become established. Bettye Hardeman suggests that "anybody just entering the business have enough savings to last for at least a year." Bettye herself gave up her apartment and moved in with her parents for her first two years in sales. She urges new agents to "Just stay in there and work, and if you do, you're going to make it. Too many people get discouraged easily and quit. If they're willing to put enough time and effort into their real estate career, they could make a success of it." Ebby Halliday advises the would-be agent to "save your money, continue making good contacts, and take your real estate courses." She too thinks the new agent will need adequate savings, at least enough "to last them six months, because it may be that long until they begin to generate income."

Phyllis Burhenn points out the importance for a newcomer of taking a thoroughly professional approach. "I was taught," she says, "that there were some basic principles which a novice must follow in order to get a good start in the business, and having no previous real estate background, I wasn't about to argue with success. You know, too many new people just die in the business because they resist a proven success system." She adds, "I just kept hanging in there when other people would probably have given up on an area. I stuck with it and continued to service my farm. Most people drop out of a farming area in about three or four months. They get bored, and many are unhappy with the slow return they get from it. My feeling has always been that if I'm not getting the results, then I'm either not working hard enough or I'm not offering enough service."

Such tenacity is absolutely necessary in the first stages of a real estate career. Nobody showed more stick-to-itiveness than Art Bartlett when he first started selling Century 21. Art explains, "You can just imagine the reaction we got when we'd ask a real estate broker for $500 to become a franchisee of Century 21. The prospect would look at us like we were crazy and say, 'Now, let me get this straight. I've been in business for thirty years and this business belonged to my father before me. We're known throughout this entire area. And what you want me to do is this: You want me to take my name off the sign and put up your brand-new name that's unknown, and you want me to pay you $500 to do that. Then you want me to pay you 6 percent on my gross revenue for the rest of my life. You know, Art, you've been out to a long lunch!" Nevertheless, Art persisted, and today Century 21 is the world's largest real estate franchisor.

What kind of people have the tenacity, enthusiasm, and commitment to be successful in real estate? They have a variety of backgrounds. Art Bartlett was a salesman for Campbell's Soup Company prior to entering the business. Mary Bell Grempler was a nurse, and Ebby Halliday operated a millinery shop. Bettye Hardeman was a dining-room-manager in an Atlanta restaurant, and Phyllis Burhenn was a secretary. That's quite a cross-section of different backgrounds! The five remaining individuals have spent their entire careers in real estate. Sam LeFrak grew up in his father's construction business. Ernest Hahn in his early twenties started remodeling storefronts. Gordon Gundaker and Ralph Pritchard began as young men selling real estate. And Harry Helmsley entered the field as an office boy. This variety of backgrounds indicates that it doesn't matter where you come from or who you are. If you're willing to pay the price, you can be successful in real estate.

But there's no room for individuals who just want to test the water. Success in real estate, as in any other profession or business, is a result of total commitment. Ebby Halliday explains, "We don't have any part-timers representing our company. We discourage anyone from going into the real estate business part-time. This is an all-consuming business. When you serve people, you've got to be available at your client's convenience. Now, that might be in the evening or the early morning; it's almost always on weekends. In order to succeed in this business, a person has to be willing to work ten to twelve hours a day. Actually, I consider the eight-to-five people the part-timers!" And Ralph Pritchard says pretty much the same thing: In real estate, the agent "has to be able to take care of the client at *his* convenience. That may well be a weekend or an evening. In real estate, you have to be available when your customer is." Ralph compares the real estate agent with a person who operates a movie theater. "There's no point in opening a movie theater at nine in the morning. Nobody's coming in. They're coming in the evenings, and that's when you've got to be there. Real estate's the same way. So there just isn't any room for a part-time agent."

For those real estate agents who wish to become brokers someday, it must be noted that the transition can be difficult. Mary Bell Grempler states, "My personal production had to be secondary to my concentration on developing other people. In those days, real estate brokers took all of the attractive listings for themselves; I decided that I shouldn't compete with my salespeople. That's a difficult transition for most people to make when they first enter the management end of the business. I found it especially hard because I enjoyed selling so much. But because I wanted to help my agents, I assigned customers to them." Ralph Pritchard had the same experience: "Without question, it's very tough to make the transition from salesman to manager." Because Ralph still recalls how difficult this was, his Thorsen Realtors makes a conscientious effort to develop agents into sales management. Ralph believes that making the right selection is vital; not all top salespersons will automatically fit into sales management.

Both in sales and in sales management, opportunities in real estate are virtually unlimited. And, contrary to what some people think, the chances for success are as great today as ever. In fact, Harry Helmsley actually got his start during the Great Depression. If it could be done then, it can be done now. These ten experts are unanimous in their belief that, despite present-day problems, the opportunities in real estate are now greater than ever.

I think I can best sum up my analysis of these ten outstanding people by saying that, one and all, *they are concerned citizens.* The fact that they care about making a profit has in no way prevented them from being actively concerned with the community at large. They demonstrate that the stereotype of the cold-hearted businessperson is a myth. As a group, successful real estate people certainly rank among this country's best citizens, dedicated to building a better America.

I am indebted to all of them for generously sharing their time and their ideas. Admittedly, when I first thought of writing this book I had serious reservations. Such busy people, I thought, might not have time for the lengthy interviews I would need. But they did find time. They were unfailingly gracious in agreeing to participate. I realized that they did so because they believed this book would be good for the real estate industry. The top people, all of whom work at a hectic pace, were 100 percent cooperative because *they care.* And it is to people with that kind of commitment that the industry owes its tremendous growth.

About the Author

Robert L. Shook has had a successful sales career since his graduation from Ohio State University in 1959. He is chairman of the board of Shook Enterprises, author of *The Entrepreneurs, Ten Greatest Salespersons* and *Winning Images,* and coauthor of *How to Be the Complete Professional Salesman* and *Total Commitment.* He lives in Columbus, Ohio, with his wife and three children.